Love

has to be the Reason

Rethinking the Formation of African Priests and Religious Today

Cornelius Uche Okeke

CONDITIONS OF SALES

DEDICATION

This book is dedicated to Directors of Priestly and Religious Formation on the African Continent and to those who organize the Formation Training Program for Africa held in Kenya.

COVER DESIGN

"The cover is the picture of vine tree with fruitful branches, and indicates that only when priests and religious develop a good relationship with Jesus Christ; the Vine, can their lives, ministries and apostolates bear abundant and good fruits"

CONTENTS

ACKNOWLEDGEMENT

Every reflection is a distillation from experiences and an on-going conversation with usually unnamed partners. My conversation partners in this book are my colleagues in the formation teams where I had served, the Holy Family Spiritual Year Centre Okpuno and Pope John Paul II Major Seminary Okpuno. The discussions I had with these formators helped to motivate the writing of this book. These colleagues and the seminarians contributed to the experiences that underlie this reflection. And I thank them all. I also thank all the candidates for the priesthood and religious life from the various congregations, I have had the privilege to accompany in their vocation journey. It has always been a journey of mutual enrichment and the thoughts expressed in this book are both gift from you and my return gift to you.

I thank Brother Anthony Shanahan of the Confraternity of the Christian Brothers (CFC). He has lived and worked in Kenya for a very long time. He holds a licentiate in psychology and works in formation. His rich knowledge and experience were brought out in his thorough criticisms and suggestions which improved the clarity and realism of the content. Sister Mary Gitau of the Institute of the Blessed Virgin Mary (IBVM) Kenya, also a psychologist, a seasoned formator and lecturer, read through the manuscript and wrote the foreword. I am very grateful. I am indebted to my bosom friend Fr. Lawrence Nwankwo for his support and encouragement. His deep knowledge of theology and culture sharpened the arguments in many sections of the book.

To the staff of GiPi publications, Abuja, Nigeria, I say a big thank you for your professional touch to this book.

Finally, I thank all the formators from various cultures of the world who labor to give their best to the candidates in the particular circumstances of Africa. I truly hope this book will be of some help in your work.

ABBREVIATIONS

APA	American Psychiatric Association
CBCN	Catholic Bishops Conference of Nigeria
CCE	Congregation for Catholic Education
DCE	Pope Benedict XVI, *Deus Caritas Est*, Encyclical, 2005.
EA	Pope John Paul II, *Ecclesia in Africa*, Post-Synodal Apostolic Exhortation 1995.
OT	Vatican II *Optatam Totius*, Decree on Priestly Formation of Vatican II, 1965.
PDV	Pope John Paul II, *Pastores Dabo Vobis*, Post-Synodal Apostolic Exhortation of 1992.

FOREWORD

The human offspring, among the animals, takes the longest to attain any measure of independence and full functioning. Except for size and plumage, a day old chick is almost as functional as the mother hen. But for the human being, long years of nurturing and education are needed before he or she attains any measure of effectiveness and efficiency as a member of the human community.

The priesthood or religious life requires special nurturing and education. Surely, it is God who calls. Sometimes this call comes through the decision of one's parents. This was the case for Samuel who was pledged to God even before he was born and brought to the temple of Shiloh at a very tender age (1 Sam. 1:10-11, 28). Samuel entered, as it were, the house of formation with Eli the high priest and his sons, Hophni and Phinehas, as the formators. Although he was daily in the house of God, Samuel still needed to respond personally to God. God came calling. But Samuel did not recognize the Lord and thought it was the high priest, Eli who was calling him. He went twice to answer Eli. The third time, Eli knew it was the Lord who was calling Samuel and guided him accordingly for this divine encounter (1 Sam. 3:1-9).

The story of Samuel captures one of the key emphases of this book. Those chosen by God to become priests and religious need formation and this is done by other human beings. The task of these formators and discernment agents is crucial and critical to the outcome of the process. It is therefore of utmost importance that the formators are themselves well formed, have an adequate understanding of their onerous responsibility and are disposed for it. Over and above providing intellectual knowledge for the candidates, they are called to use their humanity to mediate for the candidates a transformative encounter with themselves and with God.

The core emphasis of this book is that effective formation for the priesthood or religious life should be transformational. It is not about completing different stages of formation but about being transformed through these stages into those who have detached themselves from the prevalent socio-cultural values to grow a new identity centered on Jesus Christ. In the biblical tradition, the experience of the Israelites in the desert for forty years is a good image of formation. God had always been faithful to his people since the time of Abraham and Isaac. But now in *Exodus*, the time had come for God to *form his own people* through two important actions: the first was liberation from slavery. In order to become God's people, they had to be free from anything that was not God. Secondly, through intimacy and attachment to God, God made them his own people through the Covenant. He acquired them for himself out of Love (Deut 7: 7 – 8) (Oostrom, (1983, p. 28). This process was not a onetime event but a process that took time, initiated by God. This double process of detachment and attachment is what for me best summarizes what Fr. Cornelius has presented here to us as the dynamics of formation to the priesthood or consecrated life.

Formation is not an easy process, nevertheless, it is possible. It invites the one, who undertakes the journey, to fall in love with Jesus, and once this happens then everything else becomes possible. To be immersed in the Exodus process is possible – leaving behind our *"house of slavery"* for the deep attachment with Jesus based on love.

Sr. Mary Gitau (IBVM) Licentiate in Psychology
Novice Director & Lecturer
Nairobi, Kenya.

INTRODUCTION

The Vocational Atmosphere in Africa

African Catholic men and women grow up with the public image of priests and religious as persons who are offered to God. They belong to God and to the Church and, therefore, occupy a significant place in the relationship between God and human beings. Since Africans believe that the spiritual world has strong and direct influence on life in the world, it is easy to see why priests and religious men and women are respected, honoured and indeed, revered. They are seen as closer to the spiritual world than others (Nwagwu, 1993). This belief carries a price: priests and religious are expected to conduct their lives in a manner that reflects their proper place as those who mediate between the physical and spiritual worlds. The priest is at the forefront of the mission of the Church because he lives a spousal relationship to the Church, the Bride of Christ. The religious, by virtue of their consecration to Christ, carry prophetic badge before the world pointing out to the world the enduring values of the Gospel, those values that give deeper and ultimate meaning to human strivings and desires. So, African people are not wrong in according their priests and religious respect for who they are.

Today, it appears that this image of and attitude towards Catholic priests and religious men and women in the African world is changing, especially among the priests and religious themselves. While many of the lay faithful retain the image of priests and religious as people who live in-between heaven and earth, and so accord them respect, many of the priests and religious themselves have lost consciousness of the sacral space they occupy in the psyche of the people. Some take the honour and respect given to them as entitlement. They see themselves as different from the people but not in the way they ought to, that is, as men and women offered to God and who should do their best to devote themselves wholeheartedly to God and to the Gospel. Redefining the priesthood and the religious life as gateways to social privileges, many priests and religious men and women seem to be more inclined to use these vocations as ladder for the achievement of their personal ambitions and benefits. These live as if there is no deeper meaning to the priesthood or religious life apart from being their career path. Even so, career is here understood in the very negative sense. The relationship with God is given anything but the primary place and pastoral ministry is exercised without due diligence and dedication. Consequently, some priests are unavailable to the people they are supposed to lead to God; others feed on rather than feed the people with the Word of God and the sacraments. In their personal lives, some priests and consecrated men and women lie and cheat while others are financially irresponsible and unaccountable; and promiscuous in their sexual lives. While some parents and siblings of priests and religious incite and indeed encourage their sons and daughters in this redefinition of priestly and religious life, others strive to challenge their sons and daughters who are priests and religious to take seriously the vocation to which God has called them.

Human weakness, wrong motives and corrupt practices among those who serve at the sanctuary of God is not new. For example, it was Aaron the priest who received the gold rings from the people, molded the molten calf and presented it for worship to the Israelites in the desert (Ex. 32:1-5). The sons of Eli, Hophni and Phinehas, who themselves were priests at Shiloh, were described as scoundrels who cared nothing for Yahweh (1 Sam 2:12-17). Similarly, the sons of Samuel, Joel and Abijah as judges in Beersheba abused their office. The Bible describes them as "seduced by their love of money, took bribes and gave biased verdicts" (1 Sam 8:1-4). The prophetic tradition in the Old Testament has many passages outlining the sins and corruption of those called to priestly ministry. In the New Testament, it is striking that Jesus chose the 12 and his time with them could be likened to a formation program. He had to contend with the ambition of the Zebedee brothers who demanded to sit one, on his left and the other on his right in His Kingdom (Mk 10:35-40). Judas Iscariot betrayed him and Peter denied him. Just before his ascension, they showed their lack of understanding of the core message of Jesus by asking whether the time has come for the restoration of the kingdom to Israel (Acts 1:6). This lack of understanding, ambition, wrong motives and weakness among those called by God to serve at the sanctuary has continued down the ages. This, notwithstanding, there has always been great and wonderful priests and consecrated men and women in all cultures. The challenge remains to have formation process that help people to become such wonderful priests and religious despite changes in society. Presently, it seems like, in Africa as in other parts of the world, due to changes in society and the dominant values projected, many more people with the wrong motives for entering the priesthood and the consecrated life slip through the formation process and make it to the priesthood and consecrated life without these motives being corrected. As priests and consecrated men and women, their lives project the wrong motives as the right and acceptable ones.

The situation described above can be seen as evidence of decay and chaos. But I am inclined to see it as indication of a transition both in the society and in the images and ideals of the priesthood and religious life that guide the lives of people. Sometimes, things get worse before they become better if however they are handled well. My effort in this book is to contribute to offer some thoughts on how to stem the tide by calling attention to what I consider the weak links in the formation process taking the African context as reference point.

The Problematic in Context

Context is very important for understanding any human endeavor. It situates our personal and group history and discourse. It is context that provides us the problematic with which we have to deal. And it is in dealing with the problematic of our context that we evolve into better human beings, better Church, better human society. If we neglect our context, we run the risk of providing superficial analysis of the problems (if we ever notice them) or even give in to selective inattention that usually leads to oversight.

The formation of African priests and religious today has to take seriously the African context. With the increasing number of vocations to the priesthood and the religious life in some parts of Africa and its decline in others, it is even most necessary that greater care be taken in the discernment and care of these vocations. This cannot be done appropriately without serious attention to the African context and the problems that arise in it.

The problematic of the priesthood and the religious life within the African context appears to be the gradual shifting of the vocational motivation from the religious dimension where it should belong, to the realm of self-enhancement. There is a growing tendency among priests and religious not to link their choice of vocation to some religious dimension of experience, but often to their fancy and the "bright" prospects of the future. This shift is evident in the nonchalant way in which some priests and religious display a lack of spiritual sense in their vocation. It is absolutely important to recover and reinstate the spiritual basis of the priesthood and the religious life. Even the priests of the African Traditional Religion have deep respect and honor for their vocation and the God they serve. It is the sacred decorum which permeates their very being and doing that commands dignity and allegiance to their utterances.

The overwhelming number of "religious" talks, prayers, and ceremonies that fill the African continent can be deceptive. It is a significant aspect of the problematic in our context today. Indeed Africa is a continent that is religiously dense. Religion has been a great source of consolation and hope to the Africans, especially the poor and the marginalized. Yet, it needs to be noted that this apparently religious sense does not quite impact positively the socio-political condition that has kept this continent burdened by many man-made problems. A careful examination of this situation will reveal a subtle compartmentalization of life in which Christianity is sadly only one of the many other equally significant compartments. When people enter this compartment, they behave as expected. The person goes to Church, prays like every other person, and participates in the liturgical celebrations. He or she may belong to many pious societies and devotional groups. But that is it. In the village meeting or in the market, he or she may slide into another compartment where the values of the Gospel and the teachings of the Church are not acknowledged. God and the Church may be invoked and used to advance the desires and aspirations of the individual, but there is no real and effective relationship between the individual on the one hand and God and the Church, on the other.

Within this framework of religious compartmentalization, people can comfortably enter the consecrated life or the priesthood with superficial reference to God in their lives. All they seek is their comfort and personal enhancement. If they make reference to God and the values of religion, it is usually out of habit rather than out of conviction. The real world is this one in which we are; the supernatural world and the values that derive from it are not denied or clearly rejected, but it just does not have any serious effect in their lives. These priests and religious acknowledge that there is God in this world, and are even proud to identify themselves as men and women of God. But when they make choices and act, they do so as if there are no obligations imposed on them by the God they profess to serve. Gradually but steadily, many priests and religious are losing the moral credibility to challenge the social conditions that shrink life's possibilities for our people and even to point strongly to the values of the Kingdom of God. The cumulative effect of this subtle condition is that, the priests and religious, tacitly collude with the corrupt structures that oppress the people of Africa.

Another troubling phenomenon on the continent now is the proliferation of religious congregations. In Nigeria, it has reached an epidemic level, especially among the women religious. Those who had been expelled from different religious congregations and those who had left on their own, just want to found their own religious families. All it takes is to gather a group of interested young people, design a religious habit for them to wear, have some money to hire an apartment and feed them for a while before they are made to do different sorts of work to earn money for the group and finally to have a bishop willing to sponsor the group as a religious association and finally as a congregation of diocesan right. Recently, one notices a trend in Nigeria: some intending founders of religious congregations go over to Cameroon to get a bishop to sponsor them while the group continues to be formed and to do their apostolate in Nigeria.

This proliferation of religious congregations seems to be driven by a spirit of entrepreneurship and the unholy desire to become founders of religious orders. The distinguishing mark of all these religious families is their habit and not any distinctive charism. The newness of the Spirit that usually inspires founders of religious families is lacking. After all, almost all of them do the same thing. A religious once requested that her congregation be allowed into a diocese, and she was asked what their distinguishing apostolate was. All she said was: "we can do anything"! Such a response betrays an unclear sense of the identity of the religious family. One consequence of this lack of distinctive charism is the existence of so much competition among the various religious families in the apostolate because they all are doing practically the same thing, distinguished only by their names, and the colour and style of their habits.

In the present circumstances, therefore, caution needs to be exercised over the excitement concerning the many vocations to the priesthood and the religious life in certain parts of Africa. The so-called vocation boom in Africa may be deceptive, as clearly indicated in a research carried out on Igbo priests. The research showed that only 21.7% of the religious and 21.3% of the diocesan seminarians in the study had authentic ideals of the priesthood. The study also showed that a large number of these candidates have immature visions of the priestly life. For these, the priesthood is largely a place to satisfy their ego and social needs. 63.3% of the seminarians belonging to religious orders and 66.7% of the diocesan seminarians fall into this group (Okeke, 2006).

This shows that vocation boom may not necessarily indicate a real boom in Church life unless something is done to make the best of the opportunity. While this time could be described, in the words of St. Pope John Paul II, as the springtime of the Church in Africa, it is absolutely important that we, as this Church, do everything possible to harness well this windfall of the Holy Spirit. It calls for very serious attention to the formation of African priests and religious men and women. We should remind ourselves again and again that quality of the agents of evangelization is more important than the quantity. Without priests and religious men and women who are convinced of being called by God and who understand their vocation as a response of love to God who has called them to Himself and who see their life and ministry as a constant effort to grow in intimate relationship with God in the service of their brothers and sisters, the vocation boom can spell doom for the Church. The Church is taking a big risk if she has mainly men and women who are inspired by selfish ambitions, who lack the necessary human and spiritual values required by their vocation but have rather irresponsible and careerist vision of the priesthood and the religious life. This is true, not just for the Church in Africa but also for the Church in the others parts of the world.

It has therefore become necessary to raise the question of re-examining and re-thinking the formation of priests and religious men and women in Africa today. The goals and methods of formation have to be revisited from time to time, in response to the signs of the times. It may well be also that it is not clear to some formators what they are doing in the formation houses and seminaries. The result is that after the years of formation, persons come out as if they had merely passed from one stage of formation to the next without actually being *transformed* in their persons. Factors pertaining to the individual and those pertaining to the formation process itself contribute to this unfortunate situation.

The quality of formation depends heavily on the formators. Adequate and appropriate preparation of formators and their discerning involvement in the formation process are critical to the outcome of the formation process not only in Africa but all over the world. This is where the leadership of the Church in Africa is doing so badly. They are not sufficiently committed to the preparation and on-going formation of the formators. We cannot reform the formation of priests and religious in Africa without appropriately trained personnel. And it is in the hands of the leadership – bishops and superiors of religious orders – to give adequate preparation to those entrusted to the formation of the priests and religious. The Congregation for Catholic Education strongly emphasises that "every formator should have a good knowledge of the human person: his rhythms of growth; his potentials and weaknesses; and his way of living his relationship with God. Thus, it is desirable that bishops – by making use of various experiences, programs and institutions of good reputation – provide a suitable preparation in vocational pedagogy for formators" (2008, n.3). The same Sacred Congregation insists further that every formator should possess "in due measure, the sensitivity and psychological preparation that will allow him, insofar as possible, to perceive the candidate's true motivations, to discern the barriers that stop him integrating human and Christian maturity, and to pick up on any psychopathic disturbances present in the candidate"(2008, n.4).

The diocesan seminaries suffer more than the religious congregations with regard to the preparation of the formators and the vision that guide their engagement in the formation process. In most seminaries, formation is conceived largely in terms of giving lectures and keeping the seminarians under control. This is a situation we inherited from the missionaries and to which we have remained faithful, even after the Second Vatican Council and the Synod on the Formation of Priests. It is a formation situation in which popular piety can still pass off as an indicator of assimilated formation while leaving unexamined and untouched the subconscious and conscious motives which candidates bring with them to the seminaries and the formation houses.

In sum, no effective formation will be hoped for without a reasonable number of adequately prepared formators in our formation houses and the higher the number of candidates in the seminaries and other formation houses, the greater the number of trained formators needed. I will address this issue in detail later in this book.

Love has to be the Reason

Love must be the reason is the title of a song by the Christian singer, Marilla Ness. The song explains that love must be the reason for being man and wife. Love opens the hearts of a man and a woman and they come together in a relationship that lasts. This love is the reason for leaving father and mother and joining to one's spouse for the rest of one's life. This love introduces something new, something beautiful in the life of a person, and provides the reason for taking the risks involved and the pains experienced in giving oneself over to another in marriage. This love is not merely a fleeting and intoxicating emotion but an experience of something deep about the other person that results in such a radical decision as marriage. Hence St. Paul uses the image of the bond of love between a man and his wife to describe the bond of love between Christ and His bride, the Church (Eph. 5.21-33). As I argued with many examples from clinical experience in my earlier book, (Okeke, 2007) marriages entered into for other kinds of reasons have huge, mostly negative consequences.

Such should absolutely be true of those who feel called to the Catholic priesthood or to the Consecrated Life. Love, indeed, must be the reason for deciding to follow the Lord more closely either as a priest or as a religious man or woman. For it is only when love stands at the heart of priestly and religious vocations does the person respond with passion and singleness of purpose. Life is too short to be spent on something that one does not have passion for. God uses various means to call us to Him. But whatever means He uses, that means has to be attractive and motivating. He fills us with a deep yearning for Him and for the mission of the Church, just as He fills others with a deep yearning for Him that takes them to other vocations in life. In the end, it is God who calls, and our "yes" is to Him and to His work in and through the Church. The lure of Him leads to our falling in love with Him. Formation helps us respond with love to this initial inspiration of God. But it is on the basis of this felt love of God in the heart that decision to be a priest or religious man or woman is made. It is true that sometimes this motive of love may not be so clear at the time of decision; but this fundamental motivation has to be present somehow even if it is fledgling. As Carlo Maria Martini rightly affirms: "Jesus does not require a heroic act without motivation:

the promise of the kingdom precedes the command to sell what you have" (1992, p.59). It is the experience of this promise, of something deeper and greater in God, that God uses to draw us to Himself, and so, we can give up whatever it takes to get at it. It is only when a man finds the treasure that he goes and sells everything he has in order to buy the field in which the treasure is hidden (Mt. 13.44-46). The hidden treasure, the pearl of exceptional quality, is the spark of God's love that sets in motion our whole life in obedience to God and the mission of the Church. "The cross must not be chosen", insists Stefan Kiechle. "Renunciation and suffering must not be chosen because they do not constitute any values in themselves" (2005, p. 62). Whatever renunciation that is involved in the priestly or religious vocations is *because of* the relationship with God. There is a higher value which the renunciations are serving.

During a workshop on love and sexuality with a group of female novices sometime ago, I asked them what actually differentiated them from their sisters at home who were married. They said that their vocation to the religious life is special because they, unlike their married sisters, have no man they could call their husband. They said they have renounced having sexual intercourse with any man and their married sisters "are enjoying themselves", as they expressed it. I explained to them that of the two vocations – marriage and consecrated life – none is more special than the other, because they and their married sisters are supposed to have made their decision based on one experience, namely love. Every love relationship has risks and some renunciations associated with it. And come to think of it: their married sisters eke out life under the most unstable conditions in our country, and most of the time, they are unsure of food, school fees for their children, and have no concept of vacation or holiday. But as religious women, even as novices already, their needs are met, and when they profess, they will have designated time for their holidays. I suggested to them that if we actually were to do a calculus of the inherent pains, deprivations and gains in the two lifestyles, their condition would be seen to be much better than that of their married sisters. But we cannot perform such calculus because it is absolutely unnecessary. It is not important because love is the reason for the choice of any of these vocations. Every yoke is easier to bear when it is carried with love, in love and *because of* love.

They were stunned by this apparently leveling statement. They did not believe that the central motivation for the choice of the vocation is a love so strong that they could give up everything in pursuit of it. Their whole attention was focused on sex and its avoidance. And for them, that is all there is in the vocation to the consecrated life. No wonder some priests and religious often see their lives as such a terrible sacrifice imposed upon them. Yet, "it is love that can easily lead us to make sacrifices for others", and without love "simply making sacrifices might in itself just be another way of being self-centered" (Wolff, 2003, p. 65). This reminds me of a young man of twenty-eight who came to me convinced that he had vocation to the priesthood. He wanted me to help him meet the bishop who would make him a priest. He felt called to the priesthood because from his childhood he had been so quiet and alone, fearful of women, that he had remained a virgin. On further inquiry, it turned out that he had so many issues, and was even a dropout in the university. He had so many problems with himself and was unable to establish a true and stable relationship with any man or woman. He was a very lonely man. This situation had kept him a virgin, and for him, it was a sign that he was called to the priesthood!

On another occasion, I facilitated a five-day retreat for a group of postulants in a religious congregation for women. They were sixty-eight in number. To have a feel of where they were, I developed a questionnaire in which I tried to find out the reasons for their apparent willingness to embrace the vocation to the religious life. When I asked the question directly to them, almost all of them said it was God they were seeking. But when I asked the same question indirectly, these reasons emerged: fear of family responsibility, fear of childbirth, hope of acquiring higher education and of assisting their family members, unwillingness to be under any man, fear of not getting married, inability to trust men due to painful experiences of failed relationships, to continue their friendship with a seminarian, to please their parents, and because priests and religious men and women command respect in society, etc. These reasons were found in the responses of fifty-seven of these postulants. This constitutes approximately 84% of that group. A different set of reasons were found in only eleven of those postulants (16%): an experience of love of God of which nothing could satisfy other than giving oneself to God in the religious life; being converted from an old way of life and deciding to give oneself to God in gratitude; service of the poor for the sake of Jesus their love; love of the Virgin Mary, inexpressible feeling of being married to Jesus, etc.

On several occasions some seminarians have wondered why some of them are in the seminary. Discussions among them often revolve around how best to improve their financial condition especially after their ordination such as starting a healing ministry (which is in vogue in Nigeria now), how to work around their relationship with women (or men for those with homosexual tendency), find their way to those who have the power to pave their way to getting the good things of life, make all the necessary plans so that they do not have to stay too long after ordination before being sent to do graduate studies preferably in Europe and North America. Those of them who are honestly responding to what they feel in their heart about God and the Church, and are making effort, often feel confused because they are surrounded in the seminary and outside the seminary by seminarians and priests whose agenda in the priesthood come close to almost everything except God and the mission of the Church. When reference is made to God, it is usually to demonstrate one's knowledge of theology or as a deceptive strategy to manipulate the innocent and desperate masses. Without appropriate help in their confusion, some of these innocent seminarians leave the seminary. Others succeed in working through the crisis and develop a solid relationship with God and turn out to be great pastors.

What divides these two classes of Christian vocationers seems to be the presence or absence of true and personal experience of God's love which whets one's appetite for things of the spirit, for closeness with God, and which forms the ground for a kind of disposition that flows out in a ministry or apostolate that serves the people of God. This love of God is first of all experienced and then followed by the decision or choice to follow this God no matter the cost. Dolan (2000) clearly states that: "how to accept, return, and radiate that love is precisely our lifelong program of priestly formation" (p. 43). The relationship between the individual and God is then nurtured through the communication between the two, which is prayer. It is this lively prayer life that enables the Christian vocationer to make choices and decisions that deepen their relationship with God. This dynamic process is present in all relationships. In a very extensive study of the psychological and spiritual health of priests, Rossetti (2011) emphatically concludes from the results that "a priest simply cannot be a happy and effective priest without having a solid relationship to God. And this strong relationship to God is one of the major reasons they are so happy" (p. 204).

Love is the passion that drives everything we do in life. The vital question is: love for what? One enters the priesthood or religious life because there is something that is attractive in the vocation, irrespective of whether the thing that attracts one is the priesthood or religious life as it is or some distorted version of it. There is something that draws one onto that vocation path. Whatever the motivation or however mixed the motives, it has to be the passion that leads a man or woman to respond to God in a totalizing manner as a priest, religious man or woman. Our vocation to the priesthood or the religious life is concretely a response to the love of God which we feel in our hearts. When love of God is not the reason for the choice of this vocation, it is the love for other things outlined by the postulants and seminarians in the paragraphs above. Those reasons express passions also but not for priestly and religious life as they are in themselves. As many as are in the priesthood and the religious life primarily because of their attraction to a distorted version of the priesthood or religious life in Africa, so much so does the Gospel lose its cutting edge and the Church its brightness in a continent that is constantly struggling with endemic problems of corruption and grinding poverty. It is possible for God to catch us on the way and change these wrong reasons, as happened in the case of St. Vincent de Paul. But as a Church we need to do as much as we can to assist these candidates in a very gentle and loving manner in the process of purifying their intentions and redirecting their passion for the priesthood and the consecrated life, and provide them the good environment in which they can be more open to God's Word and inspiration. As it stands today, it seems to me that without a rethinking of the formation of our future priests and religious men and women so that they become persons driven by passionate love for God and for God's people, this continent will remain for a long time the synonym of all that is not working well.

Aim and Plan of the Book

This book pays particular attention to the process of formation to the priesthood and to religious life. The assumption is that formation is a transformation process both for the formator and for those being formed. The central thesis is that formation provides the individual with the opportunity to catch and stoke the fire of God's love, so that, through the agency of the formators, this individual, in response to this love of God, engages himself or herself in the process of his or her own transformation for the mission of the Church.

The book is divided into two parts. The first part has two chapters and the goal is to examine the elements and goals of formation. In the first chapter, I shall examine the nuances of the words "formation" and "transformation" in order to highlight the relationship between them in the integral human development of the candidates for the priesthood and the consecrated life. The aim is to draw the attention of formators to the need to map out the formational needs of each candidate, define the goal of the formative interventions, and develop criteria for evaluating each candidate at the end of a formative period. Chapter two concentrates on the elements and dynamics present in the formation of candidates from a particular culture.

This chapter provides the theoretical basis for understanding the challenges of forming candidates for the priesthood and the religious life in a particular culture, and draws attention to what may be lacking in our formation efforts.

The second part of this book concentrates on the issues involved in the formation of African priests and consecrated persons. Chapter three examines specific elements in African culture and how these pose challenges to the formation of Christian vocationers of African origin. In chapter four I look at the formation styles of formators and the impact they have on the candidates and on the formation process. The emphasis here is on the nature of the relationship between the formators and the candidates. In chapter five, I examine the various stages which candidates for the priesthood and the consecrated life go through, and the developmental goals and achievements expected at each stage. The last chapter is concerned with the question of discerning vocations and how important it is to take into consideration the communitarian cultures of African candidates.

Part I
Formation: Goals and Constituent Elements

Chapter One

Formation is a Process of Transformation

What Priestly and Religious Vocations are not

Any rethinking of the formation of priests and religious men and women in Africa today must go back to the roots of these precious vocations and retrieve what appears to have been lost, neglected or thrown overboard along the way. In other words, there is need to recover the inner reality of the priesthood and the religious life, both as the Church understands them and as it is also meaningful to the human beings called to live it. To do so, I consider it important to state what these vocations are not, so as to draw our attention to what are really central to them.

Ministerial priesthood and the religious life are not simply vocations in which sex and having children are avoided, superiors are obeyed blindly, and poverty is understood as a certain kind of dependency on the superior who decides on which of the requests for our needs, personal or otherwise, to grant or to turn down. Till today, despite the many documents of the Church outlining the inner reality of the priesthood and the religious life, some persons and even directors and directresses of formation, still carry a conception of the priestly and religious vocations as lives devoted to avoiding sex, blind obedience, and childish dependence on persons in positions of authority. This kind of understanding of priestly and religious vocations is both theologically wrong and

1

psychologically debilitating. It simply does not make sense. In this conception, formation becomes training in the capacity to keep oneself sexually cautious; a process for discerning conforming and dependent persons who will not give anyone trouble by asking too many questions or insisting on things being done in the right way. In a very real sense, such conceptions present the idea of formation as simply training in *adjustment* or conformity to a stultifying lifestyle. Unfortunately, it is still to be proved that such adjustment has ever worked over time in the life of any priest or religious. There could be nothing further from the truth regarding the meaning of the priestly and religious life.

Religion is the Proper Context for Understanding Christian Vocations

The inner reality of priestly and religious vocations emerges with great clarity when we situate them where they properly belong and make sense, namely in the religious context. Religion here is not to be understood simply in the sense of the cumulative tradition of a religious body which is comprised of its theology, symbols, rituals, and sacred texts (Smith, 1979). When we situate priestly and religious vocations within this context of religion as a tradition or a particular system, then we may tend to understand priestly and religious vocations in terms of institutions that simply maintain the system. While the institutional aspect of religion is implicated in the priesthood and religious life, this does not constitute their inner reality. A formation process that focuses on the institutional aspect of religion can lead to different forms of religious pathologies without transformation of persons and societies. In this concept of religion, priestly and religious vocations can easily constitute themselves as castes of power, wealth and control over others who do not belong to the sacred castes. The inner meaning of the priestly and religious vocations cannot be located here; it is located elsewhere, in a deeper and primal understanding of religion.

The deeper and primal meaning of religion is related to the deeper aspirations of humanity and of each individual human being. These yearnings seem to underlie and unify all forms of religion studied by different disciplines. Maloney (1980) aptly identifies this inner reality that animates every religion. According to him, "all 'religions' attempt to find an answer to the deepest needs and questions of men and women – birth, love, death, suffering, joy, ambition, hope, failure, depression, etc – by turning to some explanations which lie outside of a man's immediate control. In other words, they all look to some sort of transcendent principle which governs the deepest longings and experience of mankind" (p. 19). Those deepest longings of mankind are constituted by our search for the meaning of human life and of the universe. In other words, it is the longing for enduring values that give meaning, direction and purpose to human experiences; it is the longing for the Ultimate Value, the Mystery, the Holy One who is God.

The meaning of human life and the world and the enduring values that transform persons and societies, found and continues to find an eloquent answer in the incarnation, life, death and resurrection of Jesus Christ. In Jesus Christ, the groping of humanity for life, direction and meaning, finds some definite light and hope. The values he lived and taught become light shining in the darkness of human experiences and giving direction to the human search for meaning. They

3

respond definitively to the deepest longings of the human heart. In Jesus Christ, life makes an absolute sense in the midst of the good and the bad that constitute the drama of human existence. The Church, the Body of Christ, continues this mission of living and presenting these enduring values that bring about transformation in human beings and in the world.

In this context, the inner meaning of our vocation as priests and religious becomes very clear. The ministerial priest and the religious men and women are those who are in touch with the deep longings of humanity for enduring values; those who are aware of the agitations of the human heart, which are reflected in the disorder and agitations found in human society and relationships; those who find the truest response to these in the life and ministry of Jesus Christ. Theirs becomes a special call only in the sense that they live out in a radical manner these values that all people yearn for. This is the sense in which priests and religious could be called liminal people: those who live at the threshold or boundary of the human and the divine, serving as mirror to others of the enduring values of the Gospel. They are people who know personally and deeply the meaning of human struggles and doubts, and the ultimate sense of all human tragedies and successes (O'Murchu, 1999). But they have found a fundamental response in the life and teachings of Jesus of Nazareth. This is why Azevedo (1988) insists that the distinctive character of religious life "is not the vocation to holiness (which is common to all Christians) but the public profession – recognized, legitimized, and appreciated by the Church – of the will to live fully and radically the Gospel plan, coherently and as the primary objective of one's life"(p. 8). The interior and stable identity of the religious person is *that will to live fully and radically the Gospel plan, coherently and as the primary objective of one's life*. It is not the activities the religious engages in. Anyone could do any of them. It is rather this radical orientation towards God as the foundation and purpose of the whole of human existence that sets the religious apart. I agree with Azevedo (1988) that without this foundation, religious life would not exist, and would not be a justified style of life in the church.

The life of the priest as an apostle of Jesus Christ is inserted in the very radicality of the life of Jesus by which the values of the world and its promises are brought under the judgment of His person and the life He lived. In other words, the priest is not just one who doles out sacraments mechanically or one who merely carries out the administrative duties deriving from his office Okeke, 2008). A priest is one whom God has taken hold of and who has allowed himself to be won over by God's love for the sake of which he lives as a minister, a minister of God's love incarnated in the sacraments and mission of the Church.

This understanding of the deeper roots of the priestly and religious vocations has a lot of implications. First, it implies that we cannot substitute what we ARE in the context of religion with what we DO without exposing ourselves to unnecessary distortion and confusion. We must anchor ourselves solidly on what we are, which can then be expressed in what we do. Secondly, it implies that priestly and religious vocations are not merely moral adventures expressed in the vows that tend to be pursued for their own sake. Profoundly, the evangelical counsels express the state of our being rather than laws to be kept. Thirdly, formation cannot be taken to be a kind of training in *adjustment* to a way of life, but an opportunity given to an individual to reflect, discern, and grow in a personal relationship with Jesus Christ so that the life of Jesus Christ will be what

5

constitutes the foundation of his or her state of life as priest or religious. In other words, the focus of the Christian vocation is the PERSON of Jesus Christ and the encounter with God.

Transformation in Love

What are we Doing when we are Forming Others?

Every good teacher defines the scope and objectives of teaching and follows an appropriate course outline that will lead to the achievement of the goals. At the end of a period of teaching, they evaluate their students to see if the objectives have been achieved. That is why I consider it very important to raise again the question of whether we are conscious of what we are doing when we say we are forming others for the priesthood and for the religious life. We will get answer to this question by examining the root meaning of the word "formation".

The *Oxford English Dictionary*, 11th edition, gives many nuances of the verb *to form*. In the first sense, it means, to give form or shape to something; to fashion, mould something *into* a certain shape, or *after, by, from, upon*, a certain pattern or model. In this sense what seems to be at stake in the task of forming is the *conformity* of something to a specified *model*. The classical place where this kind of training of human beings happens is in the military, where the soldiers are meant *to fit into* the system without questions. The change that happens is merely a result of conditioning, even "brainwashing".

Secondly, *to form* could also mean to mould by discipline or education; to train or instruct. According to the dictionary, this usage is now rare probably because it smacks of some passivity on the part of the instructed, something that modern men and women strongly reject. However, it reflects the shaping of a person's conduct, style, *on* or *upon* a model. Again the emphasis is on *conformity*, or fitting into some model with the accent on the passivity of the recipient of the shaping.

Thirdly, *to form* also means to construct, to frame, to make or bring into existence, to produce. It implies a construction *from, of, out of* something. This usage relates to the art of creating something, which could range from the conception of ideas, to the creation of opinion or judgment. In connection with persons, it would mean making use of the native qualities or giftedness of individuals to create something new in them. Emphasis is placed on identifying the elements inherent in the person and knowing how they can be worked on to bring out something new in him/her.

In the fourth usage, *to form* implies to develop oneself, to acquire habits such as dancing habits through the practice of dancing steps, or athletics. Here the emphasis is again on building from what one has *but* through constant practice. It presupposes knowledge of what *is* in the person and *what* one aims at developing.

Lastly, *to form* means to render *fit for*, to enable persons develop certain qualities that *fit them for* certain things. Thus, we have places for the training of diplomats, or the seminary or houses of formation for the training of priests and religious men and women.

We can see that, forming people demands an understanding of formation. If we go by the first and second meanings, formation becomes a process not of transformation but of enabling people to conform well. And, as often as it is the case, the individual is not the center of formation – he or she only needs to conform to a set of standards. The formator may be a police man or woman to enforce the conformity. This idea of formation is still in vogue in many formation houses and seminaries in Africa, and can, at best, produce individuals who have gone through the years of formation without some deep changes in themselves. When they leave the formation house, the challenges of the world may overwhelm them, sometimes, to the point of confusion. The products of this kind of formation may be people who do the right thing but more out of habit than personal conviction. These are people who feel relieved when they leave the seminaries or houses of formation for their ordination or profession. They turn out to be rigid conformists who are "good" but who have no rational and personal justification for their "goodness" except that it has been what they were taught. In a situation where there are no clear guidelines on how to act, they feel at a loss. Their obedience is mechanical and their disobedience is also mechanical. *Formation of Christian vacationers therefore is not a conditioning process by which individuals are made to conform to the norms of the vocation.* Such an idea of formation will not be effective enough to produce future priests and religious men and women able to stand firm inspite of the tremors shaking the very foundations of traditional values!

The combination of the third, fourth, and the fifth meanings of the verb *to form* provides a good ground for thinking about the formation of human beings for the Church today. While it recognizes the necessity of *that-for-which-a-person-is-being-formed*, that is, a model or standard, which in our case is Jesus Christ and his gospel embodied in the values of the priesthood and the religious life, it emphasizes the importance of building *from within the person*, that is, starting with what the person has and is. *Formation, therefore, would mean the process whereby a person is enabled to develop or grow from what he/she is and has, in order to make him/her reasonably fit to serve God and humanity in the capacity of a priest or a religious.* Once this is noted, it will be easier to see its relationship with transformation.

From the same edition of the Oxford English Dictionary, the verb *to transform* means first, "to change the form of; to change into another shape or form"; secondly, "to change in character or conduct; to alter in function or nature"; and thirdly, "to undergo a change". Transformation therefore means "the action of changing in form, shape, or appearance; metamorphosis"; it is a change in character or condition. The primary idea in transformation is *change*, from one form to another or from one state to another. It is in this sense that a transformer is an apparatus that *changes* the voltage of an alternating current. Thus not only does transformation imply change, it also implies and creates a *capacity* to go on changing.

The substantive *process*, according to *The Oxford English Dictionary*, indicates "something that goes on or is carried on; a continuous action, or series of action or events; a course or method of action". In other words, *formation implies a continuous intervention in the life of a person that brings about a change because the person is capable of changing.* If we note these factors in any formation that aims at transformation of persons, then the formators should know the following elements which are intrinsic to the formation process itself and to the persons they form:

- the *focus of formation*, that is, what should change. In this case, it is who the person is, in other words, his or her personality-variables. This change is not random. It is change in the light of Jesus Christ and the demands of the diocesan priesthood or particular institute of consecrated life.

- the *capacity of the candidate to learn to change*, which implies the ability to engage him or herself in the process of self-knowledge and so be able to synthesize present experiences with past ones;
- the centrality of a *project of life*, which is the reason why the person can give up certain things in order to live that project. In broad terms, this means the values of the priestly and religious vocations. Specifically, it includes the specific charism of each congregation or the diocesan priesthood.
- being a process, *formation is continuous*. This means that the formation period is actually the initial stage of formation, which should be able to give the candidates the kind of foundation they need in order to live a life of ongoing self formation.

In other words, formation is not simply making sure that candidates keep the rules of the formation house such as being at the chapel for prayers, attending classes, keeping the rules of silence, wearing the appropriate habit and in a specified manner, taking permission before leaving the compound, going to bed at stipulated times, being respectful of others, obeying the injunctions of the formators, avoiding the opposite sex, and so on. These external things are helpful only to a limited degree. Any clever person can go through the motions and keep these external rules without being affected in the depth of his or her person. Formation that depends on these external factors may be able to keep the candidates in control, especially if their number is large, but may not effect significant changes in many of them. If formation is to be transformational, then these elements intrinsic in the formation of candidates to the priesthood and the religious life should be considered by those who form. We shall now examine these elements one by one.

Elements present in Formation

The Subject of Formation: Candidates and Formators

The focus of formation is the candidate as an individual, this unique person with specific characteristics, needs, values, and attitudes. The individual is not unique only in his or her color, height, intelligence, size of nose or the brightness of his or her teeth. These are evident and important, and they are the readily available indicators of our uniqueness. But when we relate to people, we usually go beyond these external aspects to look for those enduring aspects of the persons that reflect their tastes, their emotional tendencies, their way of looking at life and events, their basic inclinations, their values, and so on. That is why we make judgments such as: "his face is scary but his heart is gold"; "she is very beautiful but there is a scorpion in her heart"; "he is intelligent but miserly and hard to please"; "she appears to be happy but she can be manipulative"; "she hardly gets angry that people think she is dull and stupid"; "there is a wolf inside his gentle appearance, so, don't be deceived"; and so on. There are also the judgments of people and formators concerning some newly ordained or professed: "he must have learned this stubborn attitude somewhere else because he was so obedient in the seminary"; "I can't understand what happened to that sister to be so wayward because she was among the best in the novitiate"; "she is very prayerful but she causes confusion in every community she is sent"; "it is so hard to understand the puzzle in this priest: as a seminarian he was an intelligent and respectful person, but as a priest he causes trouble in every parish he is sent to"; and so on.

We hear these judgments often but we sometimes forget that they reflect our common realization that the external aspects of persons may be deceptive. Yet, the externals are the first things that attract us to or repel us from persons; they are the first things we see in persons. Our prejudices start from the impressions these externals make on us. But our experience in relationships shows us that it is very important to get to know people beyond what they present to us. Some people have suffered heartbreak because they invited people into the inner sanctuaries of their lives based on their external presentations without knowing enough of how their minds and hearts work and the values they stand for. Similarly, others have suffered terrible rejection for being misjudged because of their external condition.

Formation, therefore, should not stop at the external conditions or presentations of the candidates; it has to go down to the depth of the personality where the individual is mostly unique in his or her tastes, desires, the values he or she cherishes, the way he or she sees life, relates with people and pursues the things that he or she deems important. The depth of one's personality manifests in the choices, decisions, motivations, the likes, dislikes and the struggles of each individual. These inner aspects of a person – values, strong and less strong desires, conflicts, attitudes, – constitute the target of formation because they are the pillars on which our personalities stand. It is at this core of our personalities that we are mostly ourselves, whether we are conscious of it or not.

There is one psychological truth about all of us

which formators should be aware of, and it is this: all our attitudes, actions or behaviours are related in an intrinsic way to our personality. No single action of ours is isolated. In a certain sense, we are faithful to our personalities. We live in a way that consistently expresses our core beliefs, attitudes, desires, and needs, both the conscious and unconscious ones. This psychological affirmation expresses the metaphysical truth that every being has a fundamental unity and retains it. Everything we do, consciously or unconsciously, usually serves this unity of our personalities.

This means that everything a candidate does is saying something about the candidate's whole personality. If we want to understand the candidate and help him or her well, we must know him or her well, and not just focus on certain behaviours or attitudes as if they are isolated from the personality. For instance, if a candidate is a talkative person, it is helpful if the formator understands what the talkativeness does in the candidate's personality. The candidate may be punished for talking but that may not solve any problem. The basic question is: why does he or she talk constantly? A candidate may be talking too much as a way of drawing attention to herself. For another candidate, talking is a way of dealing with stress. Yet, for another, it is her effort to socialize. And so on. The same question applies to the one who is always quiet and appears prayerful. Is he or she really prayerful or is the apparent prayer serving another purpose for the person? A candidate works hard but sleeps most of the time in the chapel. Why? Still, there is one who is very social but unable to concentrate on anything in the formation house. The challenge of formation is to gain insight into the personality of the candidate through the behaviour presented and find ways and means of enabling the candidate realign himself or herself in the depth of his or her personality to the Gospel values.

The tendency of some formators is to target these behaviours of candidates so as to bring them into conformity with the ideal norms of the formation house. And a sign that this change has happened is when the talkative avoids talking in public or during silence hours, when the quiet person tries to make some noise. Final assessment is often based on these external behaviours: she comes to chapel on time; he does not sleep in the class again; he does his functions well. These indices of assessment are good and helpful, but to a limited degree. They can easily lead to misjudgments in favour of those whose external presentations seem to fit the ideals of the priesthood or the religious life and in disfavour of those candidates whose external presentations are suspicious. But these do not mean simply that the persons have really undergone a significant change in their lives, in the depth of their personalities, that will sustain them on the long run as priests and religious.

People change when their values, desires, needs, attitudes, are changed, because these are the foundation of their personalities. The values of the Gospel change or transform us when they challenge our own values, needs, attitudes, desires, and bring them to the obedience of Jesus Christ and the defined charism of the congregation or the vision of the life and ministry of diocesan priests. Concretely, this means that Jesus Christ and the values of the Gospel occupy a central place in our lives and become the source of our self-definition and our choices and decisions. That is why Manenti (1988) believes that the problem in Christian formation is not simply the presence or absence of faith but of the *centrality* of faith. That means that faith in Jesus Christ and His values do not stay at the periphery of the personality but at the center, so that gradually He converts everything in us to Him. It is a gradual and continuous process, but the foundation is laid during the initial formation.

An obvious prerequisite for the implementation of such a vision of formation is that the candidates be well known in their inner selves: their relevant values, needs and desires, attitudes, so that the formators can make adequate interventions that will help them. But to be able to intervene appropriately in a manner that will lead to significant change in the candidates, the formators should be able to know themselves and their weaknesses so as not to collude with the immaturity of the candidates. When a formator is largely immature, she or he can cause a lot of problems to the candidates and to the formation itself, as happened in the story that follows.

Sandra is a novice who is subservient and prayerful. She hardly disagrees with anyone or gets angry, even when her classmates make fun of her because she is thickset. Some of the novices see her as practically hypocritical and immature, especially the four assertive girls. But the novice directress likes her because she does whatever she asks her to do. The directress takes her as an example of an obedient and prayerful religious, and asks other novices to emulate her. But one day a salacious gossip breaks out in the novitiate, and Sandra is the source of it. The gossip involves the four most assertive novices, who do not appear as prayerful as Sandra, and who the directress has been unhappy with because they ask her questions. When the gossip gets to her ears, the directress, without serious investigation, seizes the opportunity to expel the four novices, keeping her 'angelic' Sandra. And her reason for expelling them is this: "they give bad examples to others because of their lack of faith. If they had faith they would not be asking too many questions". The novice directress does not like being challenged because it makes her feel inferior. How does she defend herself against this inferiority? She uses her power as the directress: she allows no person to ask her questions, and likes those who ask no questions. As long as she does not know this weakness and how it expresses itself, she will continue to be dangerous to the formation, and will tend to use the power invested on her to defend herself against real and imagined threats to her sense of self.

While the target of formation is directly the candidates in their specific characteristics, formators are also the indirect target of formation. Formators utilize the opportunity of formation to know themselves more and grow in their humanity and vocation. They should be able to assess each intervention they make in the lives of the candidates to be able to see where their own immaturity has interfered and violated the candidates' uniqueness, and be honest with themselves to accept their mistakes. Inability to do this or accept themselves and their mistakes is a sign of immaturity and very dangerous to the formation itself. If the formators are honest and take seriously their own personal growth, they should be able to be transparent to the candidates and be humble. In that way they refuse the enticement of having to resort to the use of power and authority to bend the will of the candidates. If the formators do not validate their words about personal growth and transformation with their own growth, they can be sure that they have little positive impact on the candidates. But this should not make the formators to live lives of pretence; they should be honest and transparent. Human beings are more understanding towards persons who are honest about their weaknesses and struggles than toward those who are pretentious. A formator is not one without weaknesses, but one who is aware of his weaknesses, accepts them, and makes honest and concrete efforts to grow. These qualities are necessary for a formator to be really effective.

Capacity to Change

It is not fair either to the candidate or to the Church to accept into the formation house a candidate who does not possess the capacity to change, to grow and become an authentic and joyful religious or priest. When I made this statement somewhere among some priests, some of them rebuffed me, saying that no one has the power to decide on such matters except God! Such a response does not have any real basis in reality. The call of God is always mediated and this mediation happens through the Church which consists of human beings. Otherwise, the Church would not have laid down some guidelines on how to discern vocations. Moreover, it is something that is taken for granted in all areas of life. We expect persons who are accepted into medical school to demonstrate their ability to withstand the demands of medical training. Beyond their intelligence, they must also show they can care for sick people. Those who cannot do these things may be sent away even if they are intellectual geniuses. People who are admitted to study clinical psychology must show they have the capacity to work on themselves, and the necessary intelligence to do so. Military personnel know what they are looking for in the people they recruit for training: persons able to endure the rigors and strains of military training and discipline and ready to put their lives on the line in defence of their country.

In the same way, candidates entering into Christian vocation should have the ability to grow and become genuine sisters, brothers or priests; persons with the ability to grow in their love of God so much so that God becomes central in their lives and reason to joyfully embrace priestly or religious life with its attendant demands and renunciations for the good of their brothers and sisters. They should possess certain dispositions for this kind of life. For instance, in the document *On the Use of Psychology in the Seminary,* the Congregation for the Catholic Education lists certain qualities or dispositions to be looked for in the candidates who apply to the seminary or religious houses of formation (CCE, 2008). These include:

- stable sense of one's masculine or feminine identity
- capacity to form relationship with individuals and groups in a mature way
- a solid sense of belonging
- ability to collaborate responsibly with the authority
- freedom to be attracted by the ideals of the vocation and a coherence in realizing them in daily action
- the courage to take decisions and to remain faithful to them
- capacity for self-knowledge, capacity to correct oneself, appreciation for truth, and capacity to integrate one's sexuality within the vision of the Christian vocation.

Counter-indications of this capacity, according to this document include:

- "excessive affective dependency
- disproportionate aggression
- insufficient capacity for being faithful to obligations taken on

LOVE HAS TO BE THE REASON

- insufficient capacity for establishing serene relations of openness, trust and fraternal collaboration, as well as collaboration with authority
- a sexual identity that is confused or not yet well defined"(nos. 8 & 10).

It is noteworthy that the document does not make a list of sins that should disqualify one from the vocation to the priesthood and the religious life. This is interesting because people who are called to live this life are not saints. Like all other Christians, they are sinners in constant need of God's grace. The document makes a list of those dispositions that could be described as effects of seriously wounded human development.

There is no better way to assess this capacity of a candidate than through a thorough examination of the candidate's history. Who we are today is the result of the experiences we have had and how we have managed those experiences. Our experiences shape us as much as we shape them. Because we are generally faithful to ourselves, our history brings to light what is important to us and what is not. It also indicates how we have dealt with different kinds of challenges we have faced. Through our encounter with the world, others, and God, we develop our sense of self, our vision of the world and of others; and our affective needs. Our sense of self could be more or less realistic or unrealistic. Our vision of the world and of others, could be positive, negative or even suspicious; and our affective needs could be overindulged, frustrated, or reasonably met. All these put together constitute indicators as to whether a candidate has enough strength of the self to withstand the challenges and responsibilities involved in the Christian vocation, and whether the psychological deprivations in his or her history are so deep (or excessive) as not to allow him or her develop an adequate vocational identity that will be sufficiently strong to bring him or her fulfillment as a priest of God or religious man or woman.

In concrete, the evaluation of a candidate's capacity for change, that is, the capacity to enter into the process of formation for transformation, involves knowing the following:

- What the candidate's primary values are.
- On what does his or her self-esteem rest? Is it on intelligence, beauty, attractiveness, possessions, physical strength, moral character, physique, family of origin, etc.? Is his or her joy largely dependent on how people see him or her or on how he or she sees himself or herself?
- What is the candidate's predominant emotion: anger, sadness, joy, anxiety, etc? And what is he or she usually responding to in other persons?
- What is the nature of the candidate's relationships? Does he or she tend to be withdrawn, pushy, domineering, overly submissive, dependent or controlling? And why? How does he or she take criticism? Is he or she respectful of him/herself and of others? How is this respect manifested?
- What is the candidate's attitude to work? Is he or she excited but lazy; reluctant, nonchalant, likes to command others to work. Does he or she persevere at tasks especially difficult ones or does he or she work out of fear and infantile servility, or work to be noticed and appreciated? Does he or she see work as important for human beings etc?
- How does the candidate see him/herself as a man or woman? Is he or she happy or ashamed of being male or female? Does he or she tend to feel superior in his/her gender and so regard the other gender as inferior

or oppressive? How does he or she relate with the persons of the opposite sex and persons of his or her own gender? These types of questions can lead formators to a deeper understanding of the way candidates generally think, feel, relate and work. Though no one is perfect and that is not expected of anyone, it is necessary to see that through a person's usual modes of thinking, feeling, relating and working, which are evident in the person's history, we could arrive at some positive hypothesis that such a person can engage him/herself in his/her own formation.

The Centrality of Love of God as the Project of One's Life

Pedro Arrupe, former Superior General of the Society of Jesus, wrote a very powerful summary of what I mean by a Gospel "project of life":

Nothing is more practical than finding God,

that is, falling in love in a quite absolute, final way

What you are in love with, what seizes your imagination, will affect everything.

It will decide what will get you out of bed in the morning, what you will do with your evenings, how you spend your weekends, what you read, who you know, what breaks your heart, what amazes you with joy and gratitude.

Fall in love, stay in love, it will decide everything.

As human beings we seek to live for a purpose, for a reason. It is fundamentally what we fall in love with that determines what we do and how we do it. We cannot escape it. As long as we remain human beings, we are driven by many desires till we die.

We cannot attend to these desires all at once. We notice that even nature itself does not allow us to pay attention to all the stimuli that impress themselves upon us. Hence, we develop a selective approach to life as a whole. When we try to give ourselves to everything that occurs to us or that attracts our attention, we scatter ourselves and lose focus. That is why the Igbo say that a mad person complains that his problem is that, as he is thinking and talking, other thoughts and words keep intruding and taking control! This complaint is supposed to be evidence that he is really mad, because part of what it means to be normal is that one automatically, through conscious and unconscious processes, selects what one thinks and what one talks about.

Information processing theorists hold that our cognitive apparatus develops through the process of selection and attention. What we select as important, we pay attention to. In this manner, we discard every other impression and work with those important ones. When I am studying for an exam, I give it all my attention because it is important to me. If I do not give appropriate attention to it, but rather spend time partying, I am indirectly saying that it is not so important to me. This paying attention entails doing the necessary research, getting the important materials, consulting the persons who could help me clarify confusing areas, and so on. When I am doing this in any area of my life, I am setting up a hierarchy of priorities, which will guide me through the multitude of desires and countless number of impressions that daily seek to upstage me. The same thing happens in our management of finance. We do not just spend our money on anything that catches our eyes or our fancy. Economists distinguish between needs and wants. When people are unable to distinguish what they need from what they merely want, they overspend their income, and therefore get into debt. We cannot live without priorities. The priorities constitute the values that drive our lives.

We can transpose this fact to our life as a whole. At the base of our lives is the fundamental option we have taken towards life as a whole. Everything we do derives from and leads to it. This fundamental option of our life is described as the project of life, which gives direction to all our choices and decisions.

It is important to know whether the priesthood or the religious life actually constitutes the project of life of the candidates. This is to find out the degree to which God is central in the candidate's life, and to what extent the person's proclaimed values actually play a part in his or her everyday choices and decisions. Even when a candidate appears to have the priesthood or the religious life as the driving force of his or her life, it is also necessary to find out the nature of this project. For instance, is the candidate zealous to become a priest or a religious man or woman because he or she feels that it is where he or she will make a name for himself or herself, or so that he or she will escape the pressure of marriage, or because it is an avenue that will give him or her good education and academic titles? Where is God placed in the candidate's consciousness or psyche? In other words, it is necessary to know whether the priesthood or the religious life as a project of life is reasonably objective, that is, in line with what the priesthood and the religious life actually entail and whether the choice of this project of life is free in the psyche of the candidate. Otherwise, when the priesthood or the religious life is invested with these "more personally important desires", and they are not satisfied in the vocation, the future priest or religious will definitely experience a lot of frustration in his or her life (Rulla, 1986; Kiely, 1987, 1997). Since that which drives our lives are important to us, when we do not realize them, we get frustrated and angry at ourselves and at those who we consider are the obstacles to realizing them.

What Pedro Arrupe wrote about "Falling in Love" gives us the key to knowing what constitutes the project of our life. It is that which keeps us awake, which occupies the bigger portion of our consciousness. It is that which decides why we should get up in the morning and how we spend our evenings; it determines what we pursue in our studies and the kind of friends we keep. In fact, it affects everything we do. In other words, our choices, decisions, and what we give our time and thoughts to, indicate what lies at the depth of our heart. An example: A man marries a woman primarily to make children and receive the social status of being a father. But he does not necessarily care for his wife. He is more at home with his girlfriend, who is another person's wife. Indeed his wife gave him male and female children, but the man is hardly at home with his wife. The wife receives no attention from him. His business and his girlfriend determine how he spends his time. For a priest, his primary desire is to make enough money and construct a mansion in his family. Even from the time of his apostolic experiences, he is making friends with the rich in preparation for this fundamental desire. For another, it is the search for popularity through the establishment of a prayer ministry. This desire will make him tend towards prayer manuals of Evangelical Churches, to gulp their prosperity preaching that does not include the cross and to watch the successful televangelists on the Television or Youtube in order to acquire their stage mannerisms. We can multiply examples. But in sum, what we desire is reflected in our important choices and decisions. Thus, when a candidate sets his or her eyes and heart on the objects and tasks for personal enhancement and not on true love of God and the Church embodied in the priesthood and the religious life, he or she will definitely manifest where his or her priorities lie. After all, where our heart is, there our treasure lies.

This project of life as a priest or religious should constitute the foundation of a candidate's self-definition. Anthony de Melo decries the crisis of identity among priests (and religious) so that instead of being fulfilled as simply being priests or religious, they live a kind of hyphenated identity: priest-lawyer, priest-psychologist, priest-professor, priest-accountant, priest-businessman, priest-politician, sister-nurse, sister-administrator, sister-doctor, sister-lawyer, sister-psychologist, sister-principal, sister-lecturer, etc. and so on. These other professional areas are actually meant to equip the priest or religious for the efficient proclamation of the values of the Kingdom of God. It has become so true in many places that unless a person attaches many degrees to his or her priesthood or religious life, such a person will remain sad in his or her vocation. In some countries, this situation can appropriately be described as "further-studies-syndrome" and it is driving dioceses and congregations crazy. Unfortunately, some persons in authority use this as a bait to "pull and push" those under them, a kind of "holy manipulation"! In most cases, lack of clear principles and criteria creates an unstructured situation in which personal needs and ambitions triumph over values and compete with each other. We may well learn from the profound words of Fr. Michael J. Buckley, the then Rector of the Jesuit School of Theology at Berkeley, California, who said in one of the letters he wrote to the Jesuits about to be ordained, that the collapse of the career-priesthood in the United States was simply grace of God. The reason is because through this collapse, through this crisis, "the priesthood is being called to a return to its radical, religious nature. What we are witnessing within our crisis is a restoration of the priesthood as a religious event. The priesthood is losing its secularized role, its predictable future whose initiatives and definitions are man's; no one can comfortably imagine the priest of thirty years hence and choose to be this. The future is unknown, highly ambiguous, and it cannot define the present decision. One can choose the priesthood or the religious life only through the religious experience he has now".

As the career-priesthood has been collapsing in the United States and Europe, we in Africa seem to be eager to construct one! It is not necessary to let history repeat itself. The choice of the priesthood and the religious life should be made on the basis of a religious dimension of experience because that is where they belong. It is this that constitutes it as the central project of life of priests and religious.

Formation as Continuous

The concept that captures clearly the idea of continuous or on-going formation is that of "Maintenance". Infrastructures are constantly in need of maintenance. We need also to maintain our automobiles, otherwise they will deteriorate. Our bodies also need constant maintenance, or what the medical scientists call preventive attention. When we go for annual medical check-up we are making effort at maintaining our biological system.

The idea of maintaining something presupposes the existence of a foundation. You do not maintain a building whose foundation is very shaky. The building will definitely collapse. What is required is first of all to construct the building on solid foundation. If the foundation is not strong, it has to be reinforced. I was visiting a friend in a hospital in Ekwulobia, Anambra State, Nigeria. There were cracks all over the building, and workers were digging deep holes around it. When I inquired, I was told that the foundation was falling apart and needed reinforcement. Sometimes car companies discover something that is wrong with a certain model of car, and so, they send out word to recall all those cars. The same thing applies to computer companies. Once the original structure or foundation of those machines, equipment or infrastructures is bad, they need overhaul or total fixing and not just maintenance.

When candidates are not given solid foundation during their initial formation, ongoing formation could be meaningless to them. In fact, some understand ongoing formation as further studies, waiting for final profession, getting ahead of others, getting to positions of leadership, and getting more knowledge. While these are important, they may not be vocationally helpful to a candidate who has not acquired solid vocational identity. In this sense, ongoing formation means the continuous consolidation of what has been acquired. This consolidation entails constant questioning of oneself and deeper reflection concerning one's vocation, ceaseless effort towards greater self-integration, wider readings for a deepening of understanding, conscious openness to the challenges of transition periods and readiness to reorganize one's life according to one's age in preparation for the ultimate exit at death.

It is an erroneous idea to think that ongoing formation is only for those who are temporarily professed. Some priests believe that once they are ordained, they do not need any ongoing formation. Some religious tend to see Final Profession or perpetual vows as an 'aha!' experience of being set free to do whatever they like. Even if ongoing formation is suggested to them, through seminars and workshops, the attitude of some priests and religious is often "to fulfill all righteousness"! They attend because *they have to*! They lack the zeal and the motivation to deepen their understanding of what and who they are. This is not the true meaning of ongoing formation. Though such seminars and workshops are organized at the diocesan or congregational level, every priest and religious should be able to engage in their personal ongoing formation. This is a very personal task, and each person owes it to himself or herself to avail himself or herself of every opportunity to grow in his or her vocation and humanity.

It is very important that ongoing formation should assist priests and consecrated men and women in deepening their sense of commitment and mourn the losses in their lives. We often presume that once we are ordained or profess, we have settled in our vocation. This is not totally true. The choice of Christian vocation involves the renunciation of some values that are deep-seated in the human psyche. Every decision involves some rejection of alternatives. However, it is very important that the rejected alternatives be mourned as loss. When this is not done, there are consequences. Kiechle (2005) spells them out clearly: "in the absence of mourning, there will be a tendency to cling far too long to the repudiated alternative. When this occurs, the one is never completely able to enjoy the chosen alternative. Time and again, one keeps returning to the repudiated alternative because it continues to be desired, as if it were a missed opportunity (p. 76). This lack of mourning of the losses could be at the root of the conflicting lives some priests and religious live. Without appropriate mourning, what has been rejected at the choice of the priesthood or consecrated life might not really have been let go of; it will continue to carry a significant amount of psychic energy and to generate serious conflict. And indeed, this mourning or "working through" the losses takes time and it is ongoing!

Conclusion

In this chapter, I tried to explore what we are doing when we say we are giving formation to the candidates for the priestly and religious life. Formation entails transformation of the core structures of the candidates. It means falling in love with God in a radical manner such that the relationship with God will control and affect all we do in the very details of our daily life. But such transformational formation cannot happen without proper consideration of the culture of the candidates. This is our task in the next chapter.

Chapter Two

Formation in a Culture: Dynamic Elements

In the preceding chapters, I tried to sketch the general outline of what we are doing in formation. Another important point to be raised is that the candidates being formed come from specific cultures. For formation to be effective, serious attentions needs to be given to this element.

It is generally taken for granted that priests and consecrated men and women all over the world should be formed in the same manner. It is my experience that a significant aspect of the problem experienced by African priests and religious men and women is that their culture of origin is often not considered in their formation. Often, religious congregations in Africa find it difficult to adapt their formation programs to meet the needs of African men and women. Little attention is often paid to the inner struggles of these African men and women who desire to respond fully to the love of God they feel in their hearts. In most cases, formation remains very superficial, and consists largely of giving of information or intellectual knowledge. This is generally the case in the seminaries training candidates for the diocesan priesthood. With an over-emphasis on the acquisition of philosophical and theological knowledge (which in themselves are also largely western), some candidates arrive at ordination with little change in their lives or their value system, no real internalization of the formation given to them. The result of such a situation is well articulated by the Catholic Bishops Conference of Nigeria (CBCN) in their document, *I Chose You*: "there is a growing danger of clerical arrogance, of materialism in an impoverished society, and of brazen disregard for the strategy that sustains a celibate life" (2004, no.26). Some priests live recklessly and wastefully and pass the bill over to the lay faithful who they see it as obligated to service their luxurious lives. Some priests seem to live out the unspoken conviction that they have given up raising a family of their own and therefore should be allowed to have whatever they desire. Thus, every day the priesthood and the religious life are becoming very attractive to young men and women, often not because of their singular love of God, but because of the social status they confer and the many possibilities they appear to promise. This situation is what has necessitated the writing of this book, as a call to give good formation to future priests and religious men and women.

The formation of priests and religious men and women in the African cultures today may not be very effective if African cultures are not given their full place in the understanding of the psycho-spiritual make-up of African candidates to the priesthood and the religious life. In the same document, *I Chose You*, the Catholic Bishops of Nigeria emphasize that "like all other historical beings, Nigerians respond to the gift of the priesthood against the background of their environment, cultural categories and social conventions" (2004, n. 3). If "priests are called from a certain cultural ambience", so that "the values of their social milieu affect and influence their choices and decisions" (CBCN, 2004, n. 5), then it is paramount that those entrusted with the care of these vocations know these cultural values and the challenges they pose to formation. This is true of all priests and consecrated men and women around the world.

The power of cultural ideals and values to undermine the process of formation, if not taken on board, should not be underestimated. In a research conducted on Christian vocationers (Okeke, 2003) using the Story of Imagined Future, a projective technique developed by O'Dwyer (2000), it was found out that the test was culturally sensitive. In fact, the cultural values which constitute the belief-system of the Christian vocationers were found to have the power to reinterpret the values of the Christian vocation in these cultural terms. This is understandable because, according to Manturana and Verela (1998), the foundational values or identity of every culture tends to survive any clash between two cultures. Sociologically, this is possible because the values of every culture are the categories with which the members of that culture understand and interpret the world (Berger & Luckmann, 1966). Though the human personality has certain structures that are universal it generally expresses the ideals and values of the culture of the individual. The 5th edition of the Diagnostic and Statistical Manual of Mental Disorders (DSM-V) of the American Psychiatric Association (2013) emphasizes that though there are universal signs and symptoms of certain mental disorders, care should be taken by practitioners to note the culturally specific manifestations of certain clinical syndromes: "understanding the cultural context of illness experience is essential for effective diagnostic assessment and clinical management" (p. 749). The studies of Ebigbo, Janakiramaiah & Kumaraswamy (1989) on Somatization, and Ihezue (1989) on depression found out that the manifestation of these clinical syndromes among Africans and Asians significantly differs from their manifestation among persons of European origin.

The implication of this is that it is literally of no use to impose a formation model that fails to recognize the power of the cultural values which the candidates carry with them. In this chapter, I will try to draw out the dynamic elements present in every formation to the priesthood or religious life that takes place in a particular culture and how the formators could negotiate these elements for effective formation of their candidates.

The Dynamic Elements of Formation in a Culture

Any congregation or diocese should be able to recognize and appreciate the enormity of the challenges it faces in the formation of its members as religious and as diocesan priests in a particular culture. There are four basic and interrelated elements present in the formation of any Christian vocationer, whether a religious of international or local congregation or a candidate for the diocesan priesthood. These elements include:

- the *theology* of the Christian vocation,
- the specific *charism* of the congregation/diocesan priesthood
- the *culture* of origin of the members, and
- the *personality* of the candidates which expresses the subject and her culture.

I shall now try to explore briefly these four elements.

The Theology of the Christian Vocation

The theology of the Christian vocation has guided our discussion in the previous chapter. In this section, we can only allude to salient aspects of that theology. Priestly or religious life is life that takes its bearing from the life of Jesus Christ; a life that seeks to manifest in a preeminent way the values of the Gospel and to participate in a particular way in the mission of the Church. In general, it entails a life of imitation of Jesus Christ which leads us to deeper union with God and love of the neighbor. The person drawn to the religious life or the priesthood because of the love of God he or she has experienced is seeking deeper union with the Lord. This deeper union is achieved by imitating Jesus' life and following His teachings as enunciated in the Scriptures and in the teachings of the Church. The Church continues to deepen her understanding of these vocations and provide the insights as guidelines in documents such as in the Second Vatican Council and other documents like the post-synodal apostolic exhortation of Pope John Paul II, *Pastores dabo vobis*, which is a classic document on the life and formation of priests, and *Vita Consecrata*, on the life and formation for different forms of consecrated life in the Church. These documents explain the theology of these Christian vocations and provide invaluable resources for formators.

The evangelical counsels of obedience, poverty and celibate chastity become specific means through which this union with God is concretely expressed and experienced. The goal is to cultivate a heart that is wholly given over to God in love, which becomes concretely manifest in the apostolate. Speaking to bishops, priests and deacons at Freising, Germany on September 14, 2006[1], the emeritus Pope Benedict XVI

---

[1] The address was prepared but the pope preferred to give a spontaneous reflection. However the translated text was still posted on www.http.Zenit.Org., the website that publishes news and events in the Vatican.

emphasized strongly that "to describe the priest as 'servus Christi' is to emphasize that his life has an essential 'relational connotation': With every fiber of his being he is in relation to Christ. This takes nothing away from his relation to the community, indeed it provides the foundation for it: Precisely as 'Christ's servant,' he is, 'in His name', servant of His servants". Drawn by the love of God made manifest in Jesus Christ, the priest inserts himself in the life of Jesus, sharing in his worldview, and striving to make his own the sentiments of Christ. On this solid foundation, the priest can be fruitful in his apostolate. As the Pope further emphasized in the same speech: "Generous self-giving for others is impossible without discipline and constant recovery of true faith-filled interiority. The effectiveness of pastoral action depends, ultimately, upon prayer; otherwise, service becomes empty activism".

The priest and consecrated persons grow in this union with God through constant encounter with God in prayer. It is through this prayer, as a unique value that nourishes the personal relationship with the Lord, that "faith-filled interiority" can be nurtured. In the same speech the Pope strongly stated that "the time spent in direct encounter with God in prayer can rightly be described as the pastoral priority par excellence: It is the soul's breath, without which the priest necessarily remains 'breathless,' deprived of the 'oxygen' of optimism and joy, which he needs if he is to allow himself to be sent, day by day, as a worker into the Lord's harvest".

The Charism

The general outline of Christian vocation finds expression in the specific spirituality of the diocesan priesthood and the charisms of various religious families that make up the state of life

35

described as Consecrated Life. All religious families are distinguished from each other, not simply by the colour and texture of the habit their members wear, but by the identity their charisms mediate for them and the lifestyles they inspire. Without specification by charism, diocesan priests and religious families would not have clear sense of identity. This condition will definitely have serious effect on the formation of the members. And if formation does not succeed in clarifying the identity of each religious family and state of life, it will leave behind so much confusion in the candidates.

This is a great problem in the formation of diocesan priests. So many seminarians do not know what it means to be a diocesan priest and how it is different from being a priest of a religious congregation. Some just go through the seminary nurturing many desires and aspirations which are not directly related to the life and ministry of the diocesan priest. In so doing, they set themselves up for frustration. The diocesan priest is basically the *pastor of the parish*, the one fully inserted among a specific portion of the people of God in a particular diocese. His life is completely intertwined with the life of the people of God in such a way that there is a mutual exchange of love, support, and challenge between him and the people of God in his care. The diocesan priest gives himself to this specified people, giving his life to them so that they may know the love and mercy of God deeply, and so be transformed in their lives. But he also receives life from the people of God among whom he lives and ministers (Okeke, 2009). While the monastic and religious priests form community with their fellow brothers in their communities, diocesan priests form community with their parish communities, that is, the people of God entrusted to them, and then fraternity with their brother priests. Thus, each diocesan priest is supposed to become part and parcel of the life of his parish community, and the parish community is in turn to become part and parcel of the life of her priest. The diocesan priest is emotionally and spiritually connected to the members of his parish community such that, as Rossetti notes, "their presence is an important way in which God is manifested to him" (1999, p. 35).

As I noted in the introduction, the problem of lack of a clearly defined charism is experienced in some religious congregations on the continent of Africa. This is more the case in the congregations founded recently. They do not seem to be clear about what their charisms are. There is so much confusion on this because many of these religious families are doing the same thing. Without clear specification of the distinguishing charism of the religious family, it will be difficult to channel formation towards any specific direction that will reflect the original inspiration of the founder (if there ever was any!). Specification by charism provides the candidates a clear vision to follow and the path to that vision. It seems that the problem of lack of clearly defined charism often arises because the origins of some congregations are more functional than charismatic. For example, a bishop may found or adopt an association of women and give it recognition as a religious congregation of diocesan right because he has the need to get some labour hands in the seminary or to take care of elderly priests and by extension other elderly people. This may be done irrespective of the fact that there might be other congregations with these apostolates clearly derived from their charisms. What is more problematic is that the fledgling group is compelled to branch off into other areas of the apostolate in order to have tasks for its members and to generate income. The result is a congregation that is involved in many apostolates for survival purposes. Such congregations have trouble defining a charism because they may not have one in the true sense of the word. Their existence is defined mainly by functions to be performed. To make matters worse, even the functions demand a spirituality as a meaningful anchor to the persons who feel called to the order. The functions often imply a form of spiritual life which the founder might have inchoately intuited but not thought through nor properly articulated because of the exigency of survival.

Cultural Origin of the Candidates

Every human being comes from a culture. Cultures express visions of life or worldviews, point out what is important and what is not important, what is permitted and what is not permitted, the values and ideals of what it means to be male and female, and what is considered of great value to human existence and coexistence. Through the process of socialization, all cultures insert their children into the mainstream of their cultural and social life. Members of a particular culture usually take the values and ideals of their culture as their inspiration and aspiration in life, because these constitute important elements of their self-definition.

An Igbo proverb says that however one tries to wash a pig, it will still remain a pig at its core, and that what makes a shrew, a skunk like creature, to smell is actually in its bone marrow. The same could be said of every individual: there is something of our culture that remains ingrained in our ways of thinking, acting, and expressing ourselves emotionally that does not leave us especially after our teenage years. It is therefore important to realize the power our cultural socialization has over us. No matter how we may think that we have become Africanized, or

Europeanized or Americanized, we still remain, at our very core, the products of the original culture in which we were socialized. That is why in his post-synodal apostolic exhortation, *Ecclesia in Africa*, St. Pope John Paul II told Africans to look inside themselves. "Look to the riches of your own traditions, look to the faith…. Here you will find genuine freedom; here you will find Christ who leads you to the truth"(n. 48). This exhortation from the Holy Father is recognition that every culture has great values which are seeds of Christian faith waiting to be nurtured and harvested. His statement also points to the fact that Jesus Christ desires to wear the cultural garb of every culture and speak their language, for only through this means will He bring transformation and salvation to the culture and to its members. This makes an important demand on agents of evangelization and missionaries: they should have deep knowledge of Jesus Christ and be able to differentiate their cultural expression of the Christian faith and the expression of the same Christian faith in another culture.

What has been stated in the preceding paragraphs is very relevant to the formation of Christian vacationers. Every religious family is founded in a particular culture. It necessarily wears the garb of that culture. The general theology of Christian vocation is then expressed in the language and culture of the founder. It is a delicate but absolutely necessary task to sift out what is generally the charism of a particular religious family from its cultural expression in order for it to be realized in another culture. Every genuine Christian charism is expressible in all cultures just as the ministerial priesthood could be lived by persons from all cultures. Problems arise when the cultural expression of a charism clashes with another possible cultural expression. Another source of problems is when cultural values are in conflict with the Gospel and individuals want to hold on to the cultural value, and then "rationalize" or distort the Gospel values to accommodate the cultural value. Every culture has to be challenged and purified by the Gospel. The problem can be compounded in formation if the people presenting the Gospel values are not from that culture. This makes it easy for their presentation of Gospel values and their challenge to the host culture to be perceived and framed by the candidates in formation as "cultural bias" or "prejudice" on the part of the formators. This might actually be the case. But it might also be that the candidates are using "culture" as a shield behind which to shelter from the demands of the Gospel. Sometimes, however, the founding culture tends to confuse the cultural expression of the Gospel or of a charism with the Gospel or the charism itself. This over-identification can create so much trouble and tension, especially in international congregations. In its effort to incarnate the charism in a different culture, the original culture of the founder tends to refuse some changes and adaptation. What happens often is that the candidates from the new culture are subjected to forms of treatment to make them imbibe the culture of the founder and become alienated from themselves and their native culture. Opposition to this phenomenon is regarded as indication of lack of vocation or disobedience. Yet, such opposition largely derives from what is ingrained in the psyche of these candidates. The fundamental reflection and study needed for the incarnation of a charism in a different culture are often neglected. The disposition for this incarnation is often lacking. Were it to be present, it would entail a deep knowledge of the charism as well as the host culture and a search for elements of the culture with which to express the charism. Some international congregations have endemic problems of opposition and aggression especially from members from their new host culture because of this inability to engage the culture of these candidates in dialogue. Formation will remain superficial without taking this into consideration.

Personality of the Candidates

All of us carry within ourselves the personalities originally developed from and within our cultures. The cultural values and attitudes, ethics, worldview, and human relationship, constitute the materials with which each candidate formed his or her personality prior to presenting oneself for formation. Whatever is being taught in the formation house passes through these already formed personality structures, which have their foundation in the culture in which one is brought up. The configuration of the cultural values and attitudes varies among people who come from the same culture. Each individual is different according to the strength of certain aspects of personality. Hence the Igbo people say that children may be of the same parents, but are different because each person has a personal *chi,* which is a kind of personalized creative destiny given to each person by the Supreme God at birth. This is a way of stressing the differences in our personalities. Persons are different in the way they understand things, in the way their cognition functions, in their self-perception, their relational styles, impulse management and the kind and strength of the ideals that drive their daily decisions and choices. It is these persons with their different personality traits that are the subjects of formation.

From the above, it is clear that the personality is the centre that integrates and holds all the other three vital elements in formation. The dynamics of these elements can be illustrated with the diagram below.

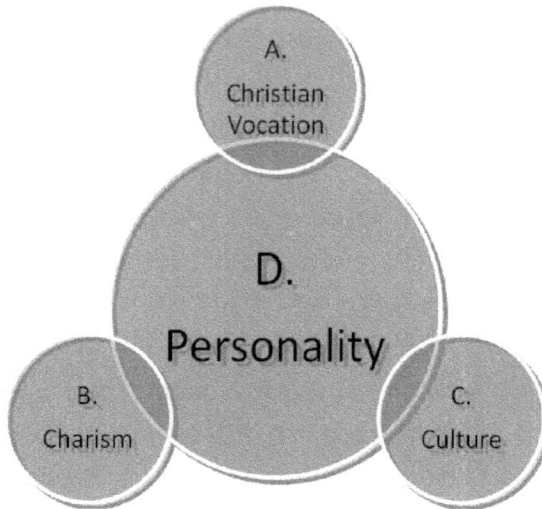

The Problem and the Challenge

The problem of many formation models has been an undue focus on imparting on the candidates the values of the Christian vocation and the charisms of the congregation, as well as the rules as stated in the constitution (A & B in the diagram above). Personality and culture were largely ignored. It took the mass exodus of priests and religious men and women in Europe and North America after the Second Vatican Council to awaken the church to the importance of the human formation of the candidates to the priesthood and the religious life. Attention began to be paid to element D, that is, to the personality. The innovative studies and theoretical formulations of Rulla (1971, 1986) and his colleagues (Rulla, Ridick & Imoda, 1978) have been of tremendous help in this regard. In the wake of clerical sexual abuse, the talk about human formation and human development has become intensified, and there is a need for careful attention to the affective maturity and presence or absence of psychological disorders in the prospective candidates. But the power of culture (Element C) in the life of the candidates is still largely underestimated.

The neglect of culture poses a great problem to the formation of candidates because every candidate to the priesthood or religious life comes from a particular culture. First of all, we accept that every Christian vocation is constituted of values to be realized. Now, these values ultimately consist in union with God through the following of Jesus Christ. This following of Jesus Christ is concretely expressed in the counsels of the gospel: poverty, obedience, and chastity. This is the general outline of all Christian vocations. These then find concrete expression in the particular charisms of each religious family and of the diocesan priesthood. These values, since they constitute the ideal which the candidates pursue, entail some challenges within the candidates and from their cultures. For this reason, the Christian vocation can become countercultural in the sense that it necessitates some radical destructing and restructuring of the persons called to follow Jesus Christ. But the understanding of this dynamic process of destructuration and restructuration implies knowledge of the structures and contents of the personalities. These have their root in the culture from which the individual comes. In the light of this, formation of the candidates for the priesthood or the religious life in a particular culture should ask itself the following questions:

- Each of the vows has a way it is understood and expressed in a culture. Thus, what is the challenge which these Gospel values pose to the culture, and to the individual's assimilation of that culture? What should be let go by each candidate as they take on the values of the Gospel?

- To what extent do the ideals of a particular culture oppose the Christian values, and what is the strength of these ideals in the personality of the candidates? The opposition often creates ruptures, for there are certain values and practices in a culture that would need purification or be outrightly dropped. This question presupposes knowledge of the cultural ideals and the personality of each vocationer.

- How do the formators verify that these necessary *ruptures* are happening or have happened in the candidates as to enable them free themselves for Christ and the congregation or the diocesan style of priestly life rather than alienating them from themselves and from their culture? How is the restructuration to be verified as taking place?

- What is the identity of the female or male in the particular culture? In other words, what are the most cherished aspirations the boys and the girls in a particular culture strive for, and how are these expressed in the candidates? How strong are these aspirations in each candidate, and how would they influence their lives as religious or priests?

- In what ways would the *ideal man* or *woman* of the culture agree or conflict with the style of life of the congregation or the diocesan priesthood?

- How would Christian growth and development in the state of life serve the full development of the candidates from a particular culture, bringing them to their fullness as men and women of a particular culture, Christian, and also of the religious family or diocesan style of life?

• And finally, but not less importantly, to what extent is the local culture in which the congregation originated ready to shed off some of its cultural trappings in order to assimilate those of the new host culture that are good? In order to respond to this question, those concerned must have insight into the dynamics of the founding culture, on the one hand and on the other hand, interest in the host culture, an appreciation of its original values, and a readiness to dialogue with it.

I raise these questions to enable the reader see where the mistakes lie in many of the formation systems adopted by some congregations, international and local, and the seminaries training priests for the diocesan priesthood. It is important to know these elements, and how they relate to and are expressed in the personality of each candidate, for these elements *constitute the essential grounds for verifying the authenticity of the person's aspiration and desires.* Emphasis on elements A and B is insufficient, and would lead to a superficial understanding of persons, and inadequate assessment of the extent the vocational values have been internalized. Some form of dialogue happens between these elements, which the individual embodies in his or her personality as mediated by his or her culture. Formation tries to help each candidate to integrate these three elements within his or her personality without suffering extreme conflicts or confusion. Dwelling extensively on elements A and B would only inform the intellect but not the whole person. The organizing center is personality (element D) which is primarily constituted by cultural values and attitudes (element C).

The implication of this is that a concerted effort has to be made to understand the culture of the candidates, the relevant cultural values and attitudes, dominant religious perceptions, and how these are configured in the personality of each candidate. Formation is not merely an adaptation exercise; it is a transformation process which utilizes what the candidates have as material for transformation into true lovers of God and servants of the Church's mission.

The Underlying Structure of the Formational Elements

These four elements are interrelated in a dynamic way, and the individual's personality is the organizing center of the four elements. However, for better understanding and for didactic purposes, I will attempt to structure them further.

The values derived from the theology of the Christian vocation and the charism of the congregation or life and ministry of the priest (Elements A & B) constitute the objective ideal to which the candidates should aspire. These form the content of what is presented to the candidates at different stages of their formation. Already, the candidates have been attracted to the priesthood and to religious life expressed in a particular religious family, and they seek to deepen their relationship with God through the practice of the counsels and a constant life of prayer. Formation offers them the occasion to deepen their understanding of these ideals embodied in the person and life of Jesus Christ so that they can love Him with all their heart, and from the interior communication established with Him, they can take up priestly ministry or the apostolate specific to their religious family.

On the other hand, the values, needs, idiosyncrasies, attitudes and modes of perception of reality, deriving from the unique personality of each candidate and his or her culture (Elements C & D) constitute the actual condition of the candidate, or what we describe as their actual self. Every individual is in the process of becoming. We always are, and are growing towards something we want to be. That which we want to be remains in the future, but is already present in our psychological world through our cognitive representation of it (Nuttin, 1985).

We have, on the one hand, the objective ideals constituted by the values embodied in the person and life of Jesus Christ and expressed in a particular state of life and on the other hand, the concrete, actual individual from a unique culture, whose uniqueness is expressed in the way in which human and cultural values, needs, attitudes, and mannerisms are configured in his or her personality. It is certain that some aspects of the values and attitudes from the culture and from the personality of each individual will agree or disagree with the demands of Jesus Christ as formulated in the theology of Christian vocation and the charism the individual feels called to live. The demands imposed by the relationship with Jesus Christ necessarily create tension in the individual which include tensions with the culture. This tension is inherent in the life of every Christian, but is expressed differently according to the state of life of each person.

As it concerns those persons called to the priesthood and the consecrated life, the following diagram describes what this tension looks like:

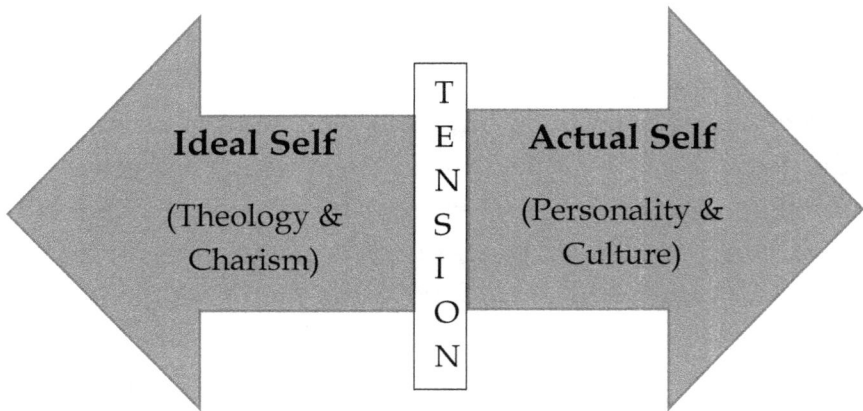

The contents and nature of this dialectical tension should be known by all formators and the tension is at two levels: the objective (the ideals, deriving from the theology and charism) and the subjective (the unique individual and the salient values of their culture of origin). I must also emphasize that the objective ideals have also a subjective aspect, which is the way the individual perceives and receives them. The same is true of the culture which has an objective form but could be differently perceived and understood by different individuals. This is why formators need to understand BOTH sides of the dialectic, and do this at both the Objective and Subjective levels. The ideal self becomes free when these objective values have become *subjective* in the motivational system of the Christian vocationer. The extent this happens is the degree the individual has appropriated or internalized them as his or her norms of conduct and the criteria for judgments and actions (Rulla, 1986). This is the reason why formators should strive to know objectively the different aspects of a particular culture and our common humanity that are in disagreement with the values of Christian vocation, and how this culture and common humanity have taken flesh in the unique personality of a candidate. Such knowledge equips the formator with what is needed for proper discernment and concrete and effective formative interventions.

It is important to emphasize that this tension between what a candidate is now, his or her concrete, actual self (product of personality and culture) *and* what he or she will be, what he or she is becoming (as a priest or religious), is the driving force of life, and should be sustained. As de Waal expresses well: "until tension enters my life I feel no need to become more than what I am. Until I am stretched I shall not grow" (1989, p. 37). This "stretching" should not be understood as a do or die affair. On the contrary, it simply indicates that we are fully who we are the more we are true to ourselves. But this fidelity to the deepest truth about us is a journey of liberation from the illusory trappings that we have surrounded ourselves with since our childhood, in the effort to find approval and love from our significant others and to belong to our important groups. When God embraces us and we experience unconditional love, we are ready to give up drinking from the leaking cisterns that hold no water of peace and joy and live for self-giving service to others (Jer. 2.13); we want to drink from the fountain of living water, which is the true God whose gentle love helps to free us from ourselves for serving His children in the Church.

Therefore, the drive that pushes and sustains this tension is the experienced love of God by which Christians seek to develop genuine friendship with God through the imitation of Jesus Christ according to their states of life. Without this passion, this drive, the tension cannot be sustained or kept alive, and therefore, growth will either be impossible or be circumvented. This tension can be circumvented or even annulled completely when a Christian vocationer settles in on one of the two poles. When a Christian vacationer settles in on the pole of the actual self, he or she follows the desires of the self and the inclinations of the ego without reference to God or the values of the Gospel. Such Christian vocationers use the priesthood and the religious life to enhance themselves, improve the lot of their families, and promote their standing in the world. Whatever will help them achieve these desires is permitted, and followed without qualms (well, there may be qualms, but these are rationalized, denied or even projected!). God and the ideals of the vocation exist as objects outside, but have no real effect on them. Their life is basically driven by their personal desires. Growth for these candidates means more acquisition of things, promotion to power, more degrees, more money, and more recognition in Church and society. In the end, they never grow to be freer interiorly in order to experience that deep peace and joy that come from the Lord, and which as apostles of Jesus Christ, they are supposed to bring to the world. The mission of the Church becomes a gigantic project of self-promotion and building oneself a secured career. The result will be much competitiveness, disregard for real ministry, struggle for and abuse of power, use of the poor to advance one's social recognition, and other evils that derive from the desire to be *somebody outstanding*!

When a Christian vocationer settles on the pole of the ideal, he or she sees these ideals as a kind of metaphysical project which rejects and denies the fragility and vulnerability of the concrete, sinful, actual self. Here, we find candidates for whom the priesthood or the religious life has become an escape from self-confrontation and self-acceptance. These vocations could be perceived as expiation grounds for the vulnerabilities of the self. These candidates are constantly carrying the burden of guilt resulting from an impossible ideal of "instant perfection" without the stain of human fragility. Since the drive is self-rejection and the goal is a neurotic clinging onto the ideal in an effortful and willful manner, these Christian vocationers do not recognize the place of grace in this journey. They are impatient with themselves as well as with every other person. The rigidity that results from this approach to the Christian vocation constitutes a block to a deepening recognition of the grace of God that accompanies us on this journey. The intense focus on the ideal is actually a denial of who they truly are. In the end it is a fruitless effort because the actual self with its vulnerabilities is always present with its imperfection. Excessive emphasis on the ideal can easily lead to self-loathing because the distance between the ideal and the vulnerable actual self could be unbearable. This attitude is not holiness at all; rather, it is a form of arrogance that doubts God's unconditional love. Such people will therefore be rigid and intolerant of human weakness when they are in ministry.

These two extremes of attitude to the tension in our lives as Christian vacationers are unhealthy. Both are built on exaggeration and unrealistic expectation of what it means to be a Christian vacationer. Relationship with God in love is the reason that drives and sustains this tension, and it is the foundation of our life as Christian vacationers. The relationship continuously challenges us to greater interior freedom to serve the Lord and the people of God. But it also awakens us to the reality of grace, that God gently leads us to Himself and to our deepest selves. It is the task of formators to know the tendency in each candidate regarding the two poles, in order to help them see how their tendency manifests itself in their daily experiences.

A Framework for Organizing Formative Tasks and Interventions

In order to enable formators be more practical in what they do in their formation, I suggest two principal areas in the life of the candidates to which they should pay careful attention. They include the belief-system and the developmental history of every candidate. Formators have the task of knowing these two aspects of each candidate so that every formative intervention they make could be reasonably channeled to the needs of each candidate. I will present only a general sketch of the two areas.

Our belief-systems have enormous influence on our attitudes and behaviours, as I indicated in the section on the centrality of a project of life. This simply reaffirms what is generally accepted as a fact, that what we believe consciously or unconsciously, shape our attitudes and behaviours. Our belief-system inclines us to think certain thoughts, to select certain impressions and leave others, and to dream certain dreams and not others. Our belief-systems contain our cherished values, the ideas that drive our everyday lives. They help us to simplify the complexities that we meet everyday. They are also a deep source of meaning and direction to everything we do. We know that we have not known a person well until we have known the values that constitute the foundation of their thinking, feeling and acting. The deep affinity in friendship is usually at this depth of belief-system. Once there is agreement at this level, other more superficial idiosyncrasies could be managed. When difference between persons and societies or cultures is at this level of belief or value-system, the difference is usually difficult to deal with. The reason is that people's belief-systems are their compass for navigating the world. Part of the reason is also that some of a person's belief-system is "unconscious", is implicit and rarely articulated in words; it is just assumed as "obvious" and so taken for granted. Thus one of the first steps is to help the person make overt and explicit what has previously been unexpressed.

I therefore reemphasize what I had already stated above, that the starting point of a candidate's ability to enter into the formation process is the kind of values that he or she has. This includes his or her ideas of the priesthood, consecrated life, and the counsels of the Gospel that constitute the dynamism of these Christian vocations. That is, how important is God in his or her life, and which of the cultural values they have imbibed will either help or impede their growth in Christian vocation. The pressure from the widespread values of secular humanism and the enticements of modern technology make it all the more urgent that formators know the kind of values their candidates have, and how these values are aligned with the love of God they feel in their hearts.

For instance, it is necessary to listen well when candidates come for spiritual direction to know from where their discourse comes. This is usually evident from the way a candidate justifies his or her ideas and actions. Formation is very effective when it is able to effect serious change in the kind of values candidates have and direct them towards the values of Jesus Christ and the mission of the Church. Did not St. Paul tell us in his letter to the Romans (12:3) that we should be transformed by the renewal of our minds? Any conversion experience must affect the cognitive level, where the original cognitive schemes (values) that were guiding a person's life are gradually transformed by the love of God and His values. Change in moral attitudes generally result from such cognitive shifts.

The second aspect includes those attitudes and behaviours that derive from the developmental histories of the candidates, which are a combination of their genetic make-up and their socialization. All human beings develop certain inclinations or habits or impulses in both negative and positive forms. These impulses or inclinations and habits seek for consistency with our value-system, so that we can experience some degree of peace with ourselves, with others and with life. When there is too much conflict between our value-system and the impulses that derive from our development, we suffer serious anxiety. The negotiation of these conflicts often leads to the erection of various defensive systems.

These impulses or tendencies, when negative, belong to what we call *human weaknesses* because they exert an influence in us towards the bad and the ugly. It is one of the reasons why, as St. Paul states, we do not act as we mean to but do things that we hate or know are wrong (Rom. 7:15). Hence, we may truly love God with all our heart and honestly strive to please the Lord and live the values of the Gospel, but somehow, the deep-seated inclinations often lead us to behaviours that are contradictory to the life chosen. As we mature in our lives and vocation, we should be able to grow in greater awareness of why we act in a certain way and work hard towards greater consistency between our values and our attitudes and behaviours. This experience of consistency between our values and our attitudes and behaviours is what is referred to as the experience of integration or wholeness. Achieving it is a task that lasts throughout life, and the personal relationship we have with God remains the unquestionable center of this process of integration as priests and religious men and women.

From this framework, two levels of formative tasks and interventions emerge: one is at the level of values (focusing on the power of the relationship with God in the person's life as well as the relevance of the Gospel values), and the other is at the level of personal history or personality which include cultural values that have become part of one's self-definition. It is possible that a person's values may be very strong and genuine, but he or she has serious conflicts that derive from personal history that make it extremely difficult for him or her to assimilate and integrate the values. While such persons do not have problems with authentic interpretation and understanding of what it means to respond to God in love as a priest or religious, they may have great difficulty integrating their experiences into their personality. Such persons, whether ordained, professed or still candidates in formation, suffer serious internal conflicts that often reflect in unstable and/or tumultuous relationships or isolation, unhealthy expression of emotions, and under-productivity, unnecessary spending of psychic energy, etc. The formative task here is that of discernment and assessment of the person's capacity to respond concretely to the invitation of God's love as a priest or religious. This is the heart of human formation.

Other persons may present a robust psychological condition but their values are totally off course. Such persons may have relational ability, good and functioning intelligence, and are reasonably at home with their emotions. But their beliefs about the values of the Christian vocation are not in sync with what these vocations entail. God and the Church do not evoke serious emotions for them nor are they perceived as strong objects of attachment. For instance, they may believe that celibacy does not include chastity or that personal autonomy should be jealously guarded against all forms of authority. The formative task here is the assessment of the strength of these values and how these persons could reconcile their beliefs and what the Church teaches about the vocation to which they are aspiring especially in its charismatic expression. In between these two extreme groups, we find persons with more or less genuine values and more or less psychological capacity for assimilating the values of the priestly and religious vocations.

These two levels of understanding formative tasks should assist the formators in situating their candidates' understanding of and attitudes towards the demands of their vocation and the pressures coming from their culture and society. Over and above all, it shows that formation is a daunting task that demands loving presence on the part of the formators, requisite knowledge, and deeply felt interest in the ministry of formation.

In the second part that follows, I shall pay attention to the issues involved in the formation of priests and religious men and women in the communitarian cultures of Africa.

Chapter Three

African Cultures in Dialogue with Christian Vocation

Every culture has its values that distinguish it from other cultures. Some of these values are in agreement with the Christian values and some are in opposition. Still, some aspects of the culture enrich Christian life and values. In this section I want to draw out a few of the cultural values which I consider relevant for the African candidates for the priesthood and the religious life. These values have positive implications as well as their shadow sides. It is the shadow side that often generates tension in the progressive internalization of the values of the Gospel. However, the intensity of the tension may vary across African cultures and individuals depending on the value's prominence in the dynamics of a person. This also should be noted by formators in different parts of the African continent.

Deep Sense of the Sacred and a Universe that is religious

Africans "have a profound religious sense, a sense of the sacred" (EA, n.42) and they live "in an intensely religious universe" (Mbiti, 1969, p. 109). Since the universe is perceived to be religious, every event and activity of Africans are understood and interpreted through this religious consciousness. There is a sense of the sacred about every situation. Writing about Nigeria, Schineller (1990) describes this situation very well: "No sharp distinction, and certainly no separation, is made between the sacred and the secular. The divine influence is felt continually, in all times and places, and not simply on holy days such as Sunday, or in holy places such as shrines. Truly we are never far from the divine and its various manifestations in the world of spirits" (p. 77). Though he writes about Nigeria, what he says seems to be equally true of most cultures in Africa. But I will invite the reader to look and see how this applies in their particular culture on the continent.

While this religious sense is a great value, it has its shadow side in the uneasiness and ubiquitous fear that Africans live in. Writing about the Igbo, Obiefuna (1985) made the case that the religious universe meant that for the Igbo, "everything has a spirit dimension in it. When we eat, the spirits are around. While we drink the spirits are around. While we sleep they are there and not a few are disturbed by spirits during sleep"(p.1). The implication of this spirit-consciousness, according to him, is constant fear. After all, "spirits are more powerful than ordinary men. Dead men who have gone to the spirit world are more powerful than men still living in this world. Men in this world who have given themselves over to the spirits by some magical rites are more powerful than ordinary people. Filled with the consciousness of these realities, the ordinary Igbo man searches everywhere for security"(Obiefuna, 1985, p. 2).

The fundamental situation is that the universe is held in balance in the struggle between good and the bad. The universe is peopled with evil and good spirits, evil and good men and women. It is believed, however, that good spirits will always triumph over the evil ones. But this does not take away the fear most Africans feel towards evil spirits and evil men and women.

This fear seems to derive from the feeling that compared to the spirits human beings are weak in the sense that they are not spirits! For this reason Africans tend to see religious practices and symbols largely in terms of worship of God and self-protection from the menace of evil spirits and evil men and women. Pious devotions thrive in the Catholic Church and religious symbols such as the crucifix and sacramentals, have also been perceived as potent ammunitions against the forces of evil and fear. Many prayer houses and different kinds of prayers circulate all the time in both Catholic and Protestant circles. When it seems that the prayers have not worked, the African still falls back to the traditional prescriptions for warding off evil and protecting himself or herself from bad people and bad spirits. The proliferation and popularization of healing ministry in many parts of Africa is linked also to this deep sense of the sacred and the religious universe in which Africans must always struggle to undo the power of evil spirits and evil men and women.

This is the universe from which the candidates for the priesthood and the religious life come. They learned their concept of God and the meaning of prayer in this universe. Candidates often enter the priesthood and the religious life with the idea of a fear inspiring God who demands many pious devotions for Him to bless and protect His people. Fulfillment of pious prayers will seem to be enough for one to feel spiritual and protected, so that entering into personal relationship with God, which effects true and concrete changes in the life of the person, is sometimes neglected. It is in this regard that the observation of the Catholic Bishops Conference of Nigeria that a magical notion of prayer prevails among some priests as leaders of liturgical worship and teachers of prayer (CBCN, 2004, n. 7) is important.

Christian religion is relational. From the beginning, God has relationship with Adam and Eve, with the patriarchs and with Israel as God's chosen people. But in Jesus Christ, God definitively enters into deeper personal relationship with humanity and with each of his children. Jesus Christ is God's eloquent statement of His undying love for every human being. Personal faith in this truth drives out all fears (I Jn. 5. 4-5). Formation of African agents of evangelization today must therefore go deeper than piety; it must challenge the candidates' idea of God, prayer, and lead them to affective relationship with the person of Jesus Christ. With a deepening relationship with Jesus Christ, the fear of evil spirits will lose its grip on the candidates. St. Paul firmly reminds Christians that by his victory through the Cross Jesus Christ despoiled the principalities and the powers and all the evil spirits and "made a public spectacle of them, leading them away in triumph by it" (Col. 2:14-15). This faith in the sovereignty of Jesus Christ should serve as a necessary foundation for the candidates to lead effective lives as men and women of God.

The Individual and the Family

Everyone agrees that family is the heart of African cultures. This family is a network that starts with the original nuclear family and extends to maternal and paternal relatives down to many generations. For the African, to be is to belong. For Schineller (1990), this interconnectedness is life to the Africans and, "loyalty to and support for one's family are primary. One is one's brother's and sister's keeper. A key image of sin is separation, isolation from family, and breaking the familial solidarity" (p. 76). But he quickly observes that "the strength of family ties can also be turned in on itself, so that the outsider receives no justice and no compassion. While providing for the welfare of close relatives and friends, one refuses to see beyond the family and to work sufficiently for the good of the state or nation" (p. 76). This is an enormous challenge for Christianity in Africa and most urgently for the formation of Christian vocationers in Africa. It seems to me that this is one of the potent reasons why the Church in Africa finds it extremely difficult to make significant contribution in building a sense of nationhood in various countries of Africa. In the majority of circumstances, ethnic sentiments overshadow what could be a broader common good.

Researches in neurophysiology have established that there is a tendency in our brain to classify objects into pairs and then "differentiate them into opposing groups"(Newberg & Waldman, 2006, p. 88). Once the brain creates this oppositional dyad it will tend to impose emotional bias on each side. Thus, "once we divide objects, people, and ideals into groups, we will tend to express a preference for one and a dislike for the others" (p. 88). According to these researchers, this is the biological root of the racial or ethnic mentality that has brought so much pain and suffering to humanity: "We are biologically prone to divide people into groups, to categorize and stereotype them, and then to evaluate them in preferential and prejudicial ways" (p. 89). This biological tendency is in service of our survival, for if the brain categorizes things and persons into components or groups, we can more easily navigate our way through the world of things and persons using the compass of these categories.

If this kind of biological determinism were all that we are in terms of human life and relationships, then there would be no possibility for any kind of cooperation between different human groups in the world. But this is not so. Even though this biological tendency exists in us, the researchers note that "the brain also has built-in mechanisms for suppressing, ignoring, or overriding" (p. 90) the perception of differences between groups. Our biological system predisposes us also to form wider relationships far and beyond our kinds and see the interconnectedness of all human beings, and so appreciate and exploit differences for the good of all. Whatever these biological dispositions, they observe that social and spiritual formations have great impact in the development of broadened understanding of human relationships.

This affirmation from neurological research highlights the revolution that Jesus Christ brought into our understanding of the bond of Divine love that holds together all human beings of all cultures, races and languages. Our families have to be experienced anew in the context of the bigger Family of God, the Church. As Scott Hahn so beautifully states it: "God gave us life in a natural family to lead us to a greater life, a larger family, a supernatural family: a family as big as God"(2002, p. 36). God's family certainly transcends "all national, tribal, and familial divisions" (p. 33). This reality of the larger family of God that embraces everyone is a central but revolutionary experience of Christianity. Only from this fundamental experience of the brotherhood of all men and women in the family of God will priests and religious men and women in Africa be able to rise above those divisive ethnic sentiments and seek for the common good of the whole people as beloved sons and daughter of the same God. Shorter (1997) believes strongly that the family remains an important model which could be used for the social reconstruction of Africa. But this will happen when Christians are taught "to relativize their own family and kinship when these loyalties conflict with the fraternal love that is practiced in the wider Church family to which they belong"(p.

38). How true this should be when it comes to priests and religious men and women in Africa!

All of us priests come from families. Our families are our first place of safety in this world. We owe a lot to our families, especially to our parents. But this does not mean that we cannot leave our families in good faith for the bigger cause of the Gospel (Lk. 14.25-33). Leaving our families does not mean forgetting them. It rather means that attachment to family should not interfere with the cause of the Gospel to which God has called us. Jesus loved his family so deeply, but when the moment came, he had to leave it to go about His father's business. He left it but still cared for His mother. He resisted every attempt by his family members to distract him from his call and mission. It is this *psychological leaving* that is most vital, and not the physical leaving.

Our family relationships should guide us outward to a broader experience of fraternity in the Church and in the world. Though a priest comes from a family, he does not belong only to his family; he belongs to the Church in which all families constitute one big family of God. "Because he belongs to Christ, the priest is radically at the service of all people: he is the minister of their salvation, their happiness and their authentic liberation, developing, in this gradual assumption of Christ's will, in prayer, in 'being heart to heart' with him"(Benedict XVI, 2009). In the same manner, a religious is leaving his or her nuclear family and relatives to enter into a larger and more embracing family that cuts across lineage, race, culture and language. Too strong an attachment to family and relatives impedes the necessary identification with the Church or religious family just as too strong an attachment to parents make it almost impossible for prospective spouses to bond with their wives and husbands. This creates the psychological crisis of belonging. A good number of priests and religious men and women do not feel the Church or their religious family is their true place of belonging. They feel alienated in the Church and their religious communities. Because of this crisis of belonging, some priests and religious men and women get into trouble with their own family members over business establishments or houses they have built either together or single-handedly. In some instances, clan members have even intervened in an effort to settle the misunderstanding between priests, religious men and women, and their family members over houses or businesses. At other times, priests and religious are so involved in their family affairs that their consciousness does not have the freedom it needs to focus on the mission given to them or settle disputes among siblings and kinsmen and women with some degree of objectivity. Some are over involved even in most trivial matters as if it is a way of asserting their authority or to remind themselves that they are not to be forgotten. A religious woman was constantly intervening in the marital lives of her sisters and brothers, issuing orders and insisting on the way things should be done, including the way her nieces and nephews should be treated. On one occasion, she had to fight with a sister-in-law over a trivial issue. The sister-in-law tore away the sister's habit and the veil, shouting at the sister that she should come home and live with them. It was such a humiliating incident, which the sister could not explain. But the root cause is obvious: family attachment.

Apart from this psychological attachment, we observe that dioceses and congregations lose a lot of their resources to the families of their priests and religious men and women. The poverty of certain congregations and dioceses in Africa is not only due to lack of income but largely due to misappropriation of Church and congregational funds for personal and family "wants". In certain countries now, it is the religious and the priests that are the hope of their family members to lift them out of poverty. Hence some people aspire to the priesthood and the religious life for this reason. Parents often make caricature of their priest-sons or religious sons and daughters for their failure to be "like that priest or sister" who has "brightened the face of their family" with money and financial wellbeing. Some have done all that is possible, both legal and illegal, to send their brothers and sisters overseas because they are priests and religious. One wonders how these priests and religious men and women make such money within the values that guide their lives as priests and religious? Some are into various forms of business, others court rich friends for their support, while others misappropriate parish or congregational funds without qualms of conscience.

In the light of the above, one of the greatest challenges international congregations and the dioceses in Africa face is how to deal with the family ties of the candidates and the loyalties that this necessitates. Some congregations arrive at some pragmatic solution to the demands of the families on their children who have answered the call to the priesthood and the religious life. Some parish rectories are filled with family members and relatives and all feed from the parish account. The provisions of Canon Law with regard to management of Church property are not well known and many dioceses have not developed mechanisms for facilitating compliance with them. In some dioceses, practices have sprung up which may be seen as enabling priests to treat Church funds as partially theirs. This is the only way one can make sense of a practice in at least one diocese I know of, in which a priest is obliged to pay up to the diocesan chancery a certain percentage of the collections without any other obligation to account for the rest. In such a situation, the priest does whatever he likes with the parish properties as long as he takes the required percentage to the chancery. Be that as it may, our concern is not whether there are policies with regard to the management of Church property or not. It is also not whether the policies are adequate or not. It is to point to the issue at the heart of the problem which is the fact that many priests and religious have not succeeded in detaching themselves and taking the required psychological distance from their families.

It is therefore important to ascertain, while they are in formation, how the candidates feel about *their own family*: what they miss in their families in becoming a religious or a diocesan priest; what kind of demands their families make on them; what and how they feel they will be able to meet those demands; what conflicts such demands impose on them; how obliged they feel towards those demands; and whether they have guilt feelings about them. All of these should be taken within the totality of a candidate's personality, his or her deepest aspirations and desires.

Unless these are known about any particular man or woman seeking to become a priest or religious, it may be difficult to help the person to get into the very depth of his or her person to address these. In moments of personal and group reflection and evaluation, candidates should be asked *to draw the practical implications of their future state of life as they relate to them and their families.* What formators should be seeking for here is the strength of the ideal of being a priest or a religious, identification with Jesus Christ and the mission of the Church, such as to give the candidates the motivational power to effect necessary detachment from their families. Every detachment implies attachment, for nature abhors a vacuum. True attachment to God and the mission of the Church can exert great power on the candidate's motivational world as to free him or her from unhealthy attachment to family. Proper assessment of this aspect of the life of the candidates should include assessment of the family's situation, the candidate's relationship to parents and siblings, the centrality of the family's image in the candidate's psyche, the candidate's conscious and unconscious comments about the unmet desires of the family, and so on. Special attention should be given to the conflicts the candidates experience towards their family and the hopes they nurture about the future benefits of the priestly or religious vocation to their family.

The Individual and the Community

A man had three daughters before his wife died. He refused to marry again. He took very good care of his three girls and willed all he had to them, except the uncultivated land in his village. But even before his death, his relatives humiliated him on many occasions, made fun of his daughters and reminded them that at their father's death, it would be clear to them that their father was a fool even unto death. The anger of the community was not that he had no male child, but that he willed all he had to his daughters. At some point, the daughters were buckling under pressure from the community and were starting to doubt the wisdom of their father's decision and to lose their sense of belonging to the community. But even on his sick bed, the father continued to assure his daughters that he was sure of the wisdom of his decision not to marry another wife when their mother was alive or to remarry after her death in order simply to have a male child to inherit his property. He told them that he did it because he loved his wife and their mother so much. He knew that every child has value, whether male or female. That was a conviction he lived for his whole life, and prayed that his daughters would learn a lesson from that. At his death, however, the first daughter could not withstand the pressure. She called the other two, and together they met their uncle, and revised some of their father's decisions. This story illustrates the tension between the individual and the community within the African cultures.

Jean Vanier, the founder of L'Arche community, makes a very personal observation: "Every time I go to Africa, I am struck by how different African cultures are from our Western culture. The main difference is the sense of community. If the image of Western society is that of the hustling, bustling city populated by competing individuals, then the contrasting image of African societies is that of the village, the embodiment of community" (1998, p. 17). This observation is so true. Every African belongs to a string of relatives, but also to the community. In fact, for the African, no one lives for himself or herself. In life and in death, African communal living is obvious. Community living runs through everything we do. We live for each other. It is for this reason that marriages, births, funerals, ordinations and professions are completely communal affairs. Everyone participates in the life of others. It provides the individual a secured sense of belonging. This is a great value and it provides the Africans the opportunity to rejoice with each other, to share their joys and sorrows. I believe it is one of the greatest protections Africans have against certain psychological problems that could have developed in the face of many difficulties they experience decade after decade. This value is so important and reflects the Pauline understanding of the Church as a Body of Christ where every part or member of the Church should "have the same concern for one another. If one part suffers, all the other parts suffer with it; if one part is honored, all the parts share its joy" (1 Cor. 12:25-26).

But, like everything human, this community living has also its shadow side. The community could weigh so heavily on the individual that it may sometimes be difficult to distinguish one's thoughts and feelings and goals from the expectations of the community. These expectations are usually both conscious and unconscious. This condition subtly rejects any form of awareness of oneself as autonomous individual who can make autonomous decisions and take responsibility for one's life. Vanier (1998) puts it well: "the price paid for such order and security is the great difficulties individuals have in freeing themselves from the power of the group, to liberate their true, deepest self, to search for the new" (p. 18). Through various measures, the community "innocently" reminds its members of the high price of losing their belonging if they happen to take a reasonable stand that challenges the community.

Though all of us yearn to belong to our various communities, this connectedness can sometimes "prevent the natural movement and evolution that we need in our lives. It can get in the way of creativity and stifle the natural loneliness that pushes us to discover something new, that pushes us closer to God" (Vanier, 1998, p. 18). Hence, an important side-effect of this communal life of Africans is that often young people do not clearly know whether what they say they want in life is their desire or the desire of their community and relatives. Since being a priest or a religious could be a boost to the community and family prestige, it often happens that the community's overwhelming support of the candidates may produce ambiguous results. The support sometimes gives rise to an obligation to reciprocate by fulfilling the desire of the candidate's family or community to have a priest or religious from their fold. Even when it becomes clear to the vocationer that the priesthood or religious life does not present the state of life one would want to live, the burden of disappointing the family, members of one's community and other supporters, weighs so heavily that the tension is sometimes resolved by the candidate suppressing his or her genuine desire. Thus, while it is good to have the support of one's family and community, formation should help the candidates free their heart from these supports so that they could enjoy them in a freer manner rather than being compelled by them. It could be the case that a candidate feels called to the priesthood or the religious life but meets great opposition and rejection from the family or community. Such opposition can be so fierce sometimes that the candidate becomes confused as to whether really he or she has the vocation. Some settle the matter by saying that if God called them, He should settle the matter Himself. Otherwise, it would indicate they were not called!

The case is different for the candidates who feel they are in the vocation not on their own accord but for the sake of their parents and community. Candidates like these feel conflicted for being in the vocation and yet unable to leave because of the social consequences. This group of candidates should be carefully handled. Sometimes, it is necessary to invite the parents or relevant relatives for enlightenment. In extreme situations, parents and community members threaten with rejection candidates who decide to leave the seminary or religious life. It can be a serious trial for such candidates. Hence, efforts should be made both at the level of the congregation and of the diocese to protect such candidates from the social pressure coming from their community and help them stand on their own convictions regarding the priesthood or the religious life. The more advanced the candidate is in the stage of formation, the worse the situation could be. This is one of the reasons why it is important to do thorough discernment at the beginning of the vocational journey. This matter will be touched again in the section dealing with the dismissal of candidates and the fear and shame that go with it.

Hierarchical Structure and the Ambivalence of Obedience

Most cultures in Africa are hierarchically structured according to the principles of gerontocracy. This structure provides a clear distinction between the old and the young, the senior and the junior, those who govern and those that are governed. This hierarchical structure has made Africa one of the continents that value old age and the elderly. From childhood, Africans know that they have to respect older people and their seniors. It is a value that makes growing old more tolerable and appreciated, unlike in some parts of the world where growing old is usually seen as sad and even shameful. This is a value that should be encouraged among candidates because it enriches the Christian message that all people are important including the elderly.

But this value has its shadow side also. Oftentimes, respect and deference is overly one-sided, from the lower to the upper part of the hierarchy, so that the older people and those who govern exercise almost absolute power on the young and their subjects. It is in the light of this that African chiefs tend to be monarchs with absolute control over their subjects, to the extent, sometimes, that their subjects could be regarded as part of their personal properties. Though a lot of changes have taken place since the time of independence of most African countries, this monarchical mindset still holds sway in Africa, both in the Church and in civil society. The pervasiveness of corruption in many African countries and the utter neglect of the populace by politicians, do not seem to be merely a lack of moral sense, but also a derivative of this mentality of the absolute power of the African chiefs.

This chieftaincy mentality plays into the hands of priests and religious men and women who invoke the Christian virtue of obedience to justify and advance their thirst for power and domination of the people of God. In a sense, some African priests see themselves as chiefs to whom their subjects owe absolute allegiance. Their theological knowledge and the spiritual position they occupy become dangerous means of exploitation of the people. It permits some of them to live extravagantly off the pains and agonies of the people and even display publicly their immaturity and irresponsibility with an air of arrogance and entitlement. After all, as chiefs and priests, no one should question what they do or call them to order, except a higher authority.

This monarchical mentality is not found only among the diocesan priests. Some superiors of men and women religious communities often live and give orders and demand absolute obedience in the same manner as African chiefs. It is not really the demand for absolute obedience that is the major issue, but the humiliation and disrespect of the persons that go with it. Power is exercised in such a manner that those who are subordinates really feel heavily the weight of the power over them.

This is simply in contradiction to the meaning of leadership as Jesus Himself teaches us. Jesus said that this kind of leadership is found only among pagans whose leaders lord it over their subjects (Mt. 20:25). But as his followers, leaders are servants (Mt. 20:26). This is where the Christian value of leadership challenges the mentality, monarchical or otherwise, that views power as what is to be exercised in the service of the leader(s) and not the led. Power is seductive, and its seduction is expressed in various forms of corruption and intimidation. It is often the collusion of this understanding of the *raison d'etre* of power in both the Christian and the political leadership that has been most effective in emptying the Church of its prophetic stance in the face of the problems that Africa as a continent faces every day.

The power that is associated with this "chieftaincy" mentality certainly creates some kind of ambivalence regarding the value of obedience. Candidates to the priesthood or religious life will tend to see themselves as aspiring to positions of power or "chieftaincy" where they will have absolute control of people under them. This fundamental attraction is stronger than their obedience to their superiors so much so that the brunt of obedience to the chieftain superior is borne for the sake of the access it gives one to exercise self-serving power in one's own little kingdom or domain.

Formation of African priests and religious men and women must reckon with this aspect of the culture. It is important therefore to examine and assess carefully how the candidates for the priesthood and the religious life understand gospel-obedience. All Christians, both the leaders and the led, are called to personal transformation in obedience to God. Gospel obedience is a great value that transforms people and society because it is basically a fundamental disposition to obey God and His Christ in and through the Church. This obedience frees each of us from the entrapment of personal and group egoism that usually breeds structures of oppression and subjugation of others.

In carrying out the assessment of candidates with regard to obedience, it is important that attention be paid to the candidate's position in the family, and the constitution of the family. Personal dynamics towards obedience will certainly differ between the candidates who are the first-, middle or last born in their families.

Conclusion

To these selected areas, formators should add other areas according to their experience and the challenges specific to the part of Africa where they work. In the following chapter I shall draw attention to the formation styles of formators in Africa and how these formation styles seem to be related to the impact of the cultural values identified in this chapter.

Chapter Four

Formators and their Formation Styles

Everyone knows that parents and teachers and formators have great impact on the lives of those under them. The impact can be negative or positive. In chapter two of this book, I stated that both the formators and candidates are targets of formation. Some formators will definitely frown at this affirmation. Yet, if we look closely at it, we will admit that it is a fact. The reason is that formation is a form of relationship between the formators and the candidates in formation. It is not so much what is said or the knowledge communicated that shapes the other. If so, a library of the best human ideals and values would be enough to form people. Rather, formation takes place mostly in the interaction between the formators and the candidates. The relationship is fundamental. If the relationship is healthy or unhealthy, it will definitely affect the formation of the candidates positively or negatively. This is why formators should be aware of how their personality and their formation styles affect the candidates and formation itself. They should also be interested in knowing the kind of relationship they establish with the candidates. This is very important because although candidates have mental representations of all their formators, they decide to let some into their inner worlds and shut others out. Those who have been shut out cannot have any significant impact on the candidate's life as regards personal and human formation. Those who are let in have a chance of modeling the priesthood or religious life for these candidates. The most unfortunate thing is for the formator to model the wrong image of the priesthood or religious life for these candidates.

Representation of the Formators in the Mind of the Candidates

We generally relate to people according to the image of them we have in our minds. If we perceive someone as mean and wicked, we assume a particular attitude when we come into contact with such a person. When someone is internally represented as manipulative, we naturally suspect all he or she says so as to avoid being manipulated.

This is how we started out our lives as children. We formed internal images of our parents and siblings and related to them accordingly. Through this process of internal representation of significant persons in our lives, we are able to establish life-giving or destructive relationships with them. This same process happens throughout our lives, but it is mostly evident in all formative environments such as families, schools, formation houses, internship situations, etc. Our internal representations of others come from our relationship with them, and this can be positive or negative.

In his *Choice Theory*, Glasser (1998) explains that each person perceives reality differently because of the differences in our "quality worlds". Quality world is a personal world which contains "pictures" of what we consider important, persons that are relevant to us, and the ways we think we can satisfy our basic needs. According to Glasser, these pictures or images fall into three categories: the people we most want to be with, the things we most want to own or experience, and the ideas or systems of belief that govern much of our behavior. In fact, Glasser affirms that "anytime we feel very good, we are choosing to behave so that someone, something, or some belief in the real world has come close to matching a picture of that person, thing, or belief in our quality worlds"(p. 45). When a person is taken into our quality world, that person becomes important to us, and can exert a lot of positive influence on our lives. When people fall in love, for instance, they take the beloved or lover into their quality world, and every day and every moment, they are looking at that image in their quality world. They want to be with their beloved or lover. When one of them falls out of that love, it means he or she has taken the other out of his or her quality world. When this happens, the power he or she used to have goes away so that the presence of that other could be irritating and unpleasant, unlike what used to be between them.

When we speak of formation as transformation process, we are implying, in the language of Glasser, that a good relationship between the formators and the candidates should be built. This will enable the candidates take the formators into their quality world, so that the formators can exert influence on their lives. To get into the quality world of the candidates, formators need to give the candidates the necessary and trusting atmosphere to share themselves freely and be listened to. Without this good and trusting relationship, formators can mostly depend on what they teach in words, which, at best, will increase the intellectual knowledge of the candidates but will most probably not effect a qualitative change in their lives. *Formation actually is happening when the person of Jesus and the values he proclaimed become real in the quality world of the candidates through the mediation of the relationship between the candidates and their formators.* It is ineffective for formators to lecture the candidates on how, for instance, Jesus respects the freedom and uniqueness of each of his disciples, but they, the formators, do not have any regard for the uniqueness and difference of each of the candidates. The candidates will take this as a theoretical truth, which may have no basis in reality. What this means is that this truth which is known by the intellect does not carry much of an emotion for the candidate as to impact positively on the way he or she relates with others. It will therefore be necessary for formators to review their formation styles and be interested in knowing how they come across to the candidates under their care.

Formation Styles and their Implications

I chose to describe this section as formation styles, because the emphasis is on the personality needs of the formators, which underlie the formation style they are inclined to adopt. Some authors (Arbuckle, 1996; Okeke, 2006) have talked about formation methods and based their classification on the differences in theoretical understanding of the meaning and goal of formation. Classification of formation styles that focuses attention on the personality needs of the formators is meant to complement the classification based on methods. However, the classification and description of formation styles is also aimed at helping the formators to look at themselves more closely and objectively and be able to assess how their personality needs could be impacting positively or negatively on the formative process. This classification came from extensive observation carried out in various formation houses and seminaries.

Authoritarian or Military Style

This style is mostly adopted by formators who have strong need for control. This style seems to be very widespread in formation houses and seminaries in Africa. Formators who use an authoritarian style are preoccupied with the conformity of the candidates to the rules and regulations of the formation house. The authoritarian formator is interested in the unquestionable submission of the candidates to his or her dictates and can use any means to achieve this goal. It emphasizes the gap between the candidates and the formators, insisting that this gap should be maintained unquestionably through the attitude of submissiveness. They use intimidation and verbal humiliation to coerce the candidates to submission. Physical punishment is sometimes employed. Some other forms of physical punishment are used, such as standing on one foot for some period of time. Whatever can be used to bend the will of the candidates to conformity is used.

In some formation houses where this style is predominant, the formators constantly remind the candidates that they (the formators) have the power to decide whether they should proceed to ordination or profession. This reminder is a manipulative strategy designed to achieve the goal of control. At one level, the authoritarian formator is usually filled with a sense of power and authority. But at another level, underneath the surface the authoritarian person is often filled with fear and inadequacy. To paper over this feeling of inadequacy, the authoritarian formator exercises power in a manner that will make the candidates feel the weight of it. For the authoritarian formator, there is no room for dialogue with the candidates, who are considered not well informed or inexperienced or simply "children" who could be unruly. All learning must come from the formators, and nothing could be learned from the candidates.

Authoritarian or military style of formation is one that turns the formation house into a system of control through mental and physical means. The value of respect for elders in African culture is often invoked to support the authoritarian formator's need for absolute control of the candidates. It is a submission that does not need reason. Personal opinions of the candidates are generally suppressed. In some places, expression of personal opinion or asking of questions is considered a tendency to disobey. The uniqueness of individuals is generally rejected in favour of general rules and behaviours. The authoritarian formator enjoys the fear and anxiety he or she instills in the candidates and interprets it as respect. In some houses of formation where this style of formation is used, some candidates, especially females, tend to deal with the constant tension through somatization – the projection of psychic uneasiness and tension on the body. Such candidates are often sick and are rarely completely well for long.

This style of formation generally produces conformists, children in adult bodies, who may be lacking in responsible attention to the challenges of their apostolate. Those so formed also tend to lack in personal initiative since they were not challenged enough to think and behave like responsible adults during the period of initial formation. When these persons become formators or are placed in charge of others, most of them become authoritarian and invoke the same reasons of obedience and seniority to justify their authoritarian attitudes and actions. Those of them in charge of the temporary professed become terrors to those under them.

The most devastating effect of this style is that the emphasis placed on conformity and submissiveness does not allow the candidates to digest, reflect on and think about what they learn in formation. Internalization of the values of the vocation becomes difficult. Most of the time, candidates arrive at ordination, first profession or final profession with a lot of anger and rebelliousness. Unless they deal with those emotional issues, some of these priests and religious men and women end up being too rebellious and critical of all persons in authority; others end up in depression, having lost the will to express themselves. Candidates who use unquestioning submissiveness to get approval succeed in this kind of formation because they will always do what they are asked to do. They usually are the favoured of the authoritarian formators and are held up as models to the others. Yet, after ordination or profession, their incompetence often shows itself. Since they are dependent on the thinking and direction of persons in authority, they find it difficult to deal with any emergency situation which tasks their initiative and practical wisdom (*phronesis*) which enables one to carefully weigh options where no clear directive exists or can exist so as to decide on the best course of action. Responsibility easily overwhelms them.

As could be seen, the authoritarian formation style is largely counterproductive. It produces emotionally repressed and potentially rebellious priests and religious men and women. It also provides the opportunity for the clever ones to manipulate their way through the system. But above all, the authoritarian formator is more focused on the satisfaction of his or her need of control (and love) than on the candidates' growth. This is a fundamental problem. Indeed, persons with excessive need for control and love should not really work in the formation house. It is necessary for them to work through these strong needs which, usually mask deep-seated feeling of inferiority. If they have to work in formation, they need to work on themselves and constantly evaluate their relationship with the candidates because they tend to love only those who obey and adore them sheepishly. In some cases, they should be honest with themselves and decline working in the formation apostolate.

Indulgent Style

This style is mostly adopted by formators who are too needy. I have also observed that those formators who love pleasure and detest any pain and discipline in their lives, are inclined to adopt this style of formation. They lack firmness and a sense of objectivity as to what is right and what is wrong. Maintaining order and rules is painful to them because often they do not have the energy for that. Moreover, doing this will question their self-indulgent lifestyle and crave for good times for themselves. Fearing any inhibition to their own desires and needs, they allow the candidates to do whatever they like because challenging them or calling them to discipline could endanger his or her need for love and freedom.

These formators become "mother" or "father" Christmas to the candidates. There are no established criteria of discernment because "only God can judge people", they reason. The concept of mediation is toyed with and the formation house can be turned into a party ground where people are permitted to pursue whatever they want. The candidates are encouraged to catch up with their counterparts in the society in following the latest fashion in almost everything provided it makes them happy. In this way, the indulgent formator is justified in his or her own undisciplined life of pleasure and lack of inhibition. Like children in the kindergarten the candidates compete over who will get the greater love of the master or mistress. It is a haven, a brave new world where life is always sunny and the death of Christ has taken away all our tears and sorrows. The Christian vocation is a life of glory without cross.

Indulgent formators tend to be impulsive and lack a clear sense of boundaries. They do not care about what they say, where and how they say it. Whatever they feel like doing, they go on with that.

In one novitiate, the indulgent novice mistress chose from the novices two beautiful girls who would be giving her massage every evening, with her two feet dipped in a bowl of warm water. According to her, the massage was meant to help her sleep well, and she considered it more helpful than taking medication. For her, it was what she wanted, and there was nothing wrong with that. The two novices saw themselves as privileged to do this "sacred duty" to their "mama"! Each time the assistant mistress called the attention of the novice mistress to the increasingly *laissez-faire* attitude in the formation house, the novice mistress would caution the assistant, telling her that "the girls should be allowed to be themselves", and that "I do not want any stress in my life"! An observant visitor would notice the unkempt nature of the compound and how disorderly things were in that novitiate. The novices always *appeared* happy except those who felt there was no order in the formation house.

Formators who use this style tend to be popular with the candidates because they allow the candidates to follow their desires. Children are always happy with the parent who indulges their desires without question. However, this style of formation tends to produce priests or religious men and women who tend to be highly irresponsible, selfish and exploitative of every situation in which they find themselves. Their sense of vocation and mission is determined by what will make them happy and comfortable. The idea of sacrifice and commitment is lost. They generally do not have a sense of community, whether of the Church, diocese or congregation. They simply think of themselves and what any situation can offer them to achieve personal goals and desires. Whatever does not have reference to the self does not have much value for such people.

However, those candidates who are responsibly independent thrive in this kind of formation environment. They grow, not so much by the impact of the formator who appears irresponsible to them, but by their appropriate use of the freedom in the environment. They utilize the freedom to think their own thoughts, ask serious questions that lead them to personal conviction regarding their vocational commitment. These can articulate genuine and personal explanations for the life they want to live. These candidates actually form themselves by using the freedom in the environment to their advantage. They usually turn out to be personally responsible and convinced individuals for whom their vocation has personal meaning.

Indulgent formators represent degenerate secular humanism in the formation houses. They give the candidates false promises and a lofty idea of the Christian vocation. But they fail in helping the candidates imbibe the discipline needed to rise up to it. Indulgent formators set up candidates for frustration in the future, when they are not allowed to follow their desires as and when they want to. In the long run, indulgent formators are a disaster in formation. That is why it is important to know whom to select for the work of formation.

The Mystification Style

Formators who adopt this style of formation are usually so insecure in themselves that they do not allow the students to know them. They are very self-protective. Withdrawal from personal contact with the candidates is a way of hiding and keeping their insecurity to themselves. It protects them from being vulnerable before the candidates. They maintain a stone-face, a show-no-emotions stance. They develop a sense of mystery around themselves. Through this mystification, they keep the candidates away from them. Standing before them feels like being surrounded by uncertainty and unpredictability. Through this mystification, they exercise enormous power and control over the candidates. Not knowing how the formator would act or feel about issues, the candidates are often at a loss. Candidates spend more time and energy trying to figure out the mystery around the formator than engaging themselves in the formation. A genuine relationship is hard to build with the mystifying formator. And indeed, he or she does not need these relationships, which entail some degree of vulnerability and openness which can be risky and unpredictable.

Formators who deploy the mystification strategy often use non-verbal ways of communication. They only need to turn their faces in a certain way, take a certain posture, or glance in a particular way. If they happen to use words to communicate, it is minimal and will lack emotion. They are very formal and usually stern.

Candidates under such a formator always feel confused and uncertain as to how to act. They are afraid, but not clear about what they are afraid of. The candidates will always have to struggle to interpret the signals given by the formator. In a workshop held with candidates and a formator who used this style, the candidates complained that it was not easy for them to know when they were doing the right or wrong thing. In most cases, the formator would not say anything. They were wondering whether she expected them to know everything. All that the formator could reply to such a challenge was that the candidates should not be worried about what pleased her or not. They should pay attention to their formation. The candidates pleaded that the formator would communicate more in words than in signs.

This style of formation could produce priests, religious men and women who may be emotionally disengaged from others and uncertain about openness. This disposition is not helpful for healthy community living as religious, and it works against the pastoral presence expected of a pastor in a parish setting. It encourages the use of nonverbal ways of expressing oneself rather than verbal means. In community meetings, persons like this say very little, but what they want to do is in their minds. They will expect others to read the signs they give out and *see* with them. People like this become an emotional burden to the community. With such a priest in a parish setting, the parishioners hardly know what he wants. They will grow tired of making efforts to know "what our priest wants from us". The people will make effort to have an affective connection to him but that will be difficult because he distances himself emotionally from them. In some cases, too, he is not physically available. Being unavailable physically and emotionally can become frustrating to the people under his care. He does his duties, but that is it! The more the parishioners look, the less they see and understand who he is!

Authoritative Style

Formators that are authoritative combine gentility, love and respect for individuals, with firmness in formation. Such formators have really grown in their humanity and vocational commitment. The principles of formation are reasonably clear to them and they try as much as possible to implement them and pass them on to the candidates, but with love and respect. They believe that individuals are different and make effort to understand them in their differences and age-related challenges. They have time for dialogue, and consider the opinion of the candidates. They do not simply spell out the rules and regulations to the candidates; they rather try to make the rules and regulations clear and persuasive to the candidates. They constantly appeal to the freedom of the candidates to make responsible choice of what is good and right for them and for the formation environment.

The goal of authoritative style is the formation of individuals who should feel responsible for themselves, for the choice they are trying to make, and for the Church they feel called to serve. The candidates know that the authoritative formator loves them. But they also know that this love is not mere sentiment, but a kind of *tough love*, which challenges the candidates to rise up to the challenges of their vocation and of their commitment.

The formator who uses authoritative style of formation focuses attention on the needs of the candidates in formation rather than on his or her needs. Such a formator is conscious of when and how he or she tends to violate the candidates through his or her own needs and reactions. And he or she does not feel humiliated to apologize when this happens. Through this mutual relationship, a great bond is created between the formator and the candidates. The trust between the formator and candidates enables the candidates to challenge themselves and be more open to their formator so that they can be helped.

Formators with this style are very few in number. But in all the formation houses where they are found, one observes a remarkable ability, responsible assertiveness, freedom, self-respect, and a high sense of responsibility in many of the candidates. One thing that is so obvious is the complete absence of threat or intimidation of any kind. It seems to me that the sense of self-respect which this style communicates to the candidates enables them to question themselves honestly regarding their vocation and their readiness to commit themselves to it. Even with those candidates who always prefer to manipulate themselves and the formation environment, this formation style makes them see that their future lives will be the cumulative effect of the manipulative choices they have made today. In other words, they are responsible even for choosing to manipulate themselves through the formative program. At every available opportunity, the authoritative formators put it before the candidates that they (the candidates) are responsible for their lives and for the mission of Christ and His Church to be entrusted to their care.

Authoritative formators acknowledge that candidates actually form them too. Since no one is fully formed, they are also open to formation. They learn about themselves from their reactions to the candidates and to various situations. Some of these formators have colleagues they dialogue with about the events in the formation house – could be someone they are living with or someone outside the formation house. Such dialogues provide the space in which the formators look at themselves, learn more about themselves, examine how they feel towards particular candidates and evaluate the interventions they made on the candidates within the period. In this way, they engage themselves in formation too. As they grow in self-knowledge, they are more enabled to help the candidates in their growth process.

It is obvious that formators with this formation style will definitely have more positive and lasting impact on the candidates. They try to engage the candidates in such a way as to change the structures on which their personalities are built. This change must happen from within, and is not imposed from outside. Such formators dispose the candidates to consider the reasonability of the Christian vocation and challenge the candidates to assess their own capacity to follow the Divine Master who has called them in love and to rise up to the consequences of saying yes to this call. When it is obvious that it will be extremely difficult for a candidate to live according to the demands of the vocation, the authoritative formator does not hide it from the candidate. He or she calls the candidate and explains everything to him or her. Though usually difficult to accept, the authoritative formator will always insist, however paradoxical this may sound, that the candidate goes home for the candidate's "own good".

Formators who adopt authoritative style of formation have largely grown in their personalities. It does not mean they do not have weaknesses. Rather, they have reasonably made peace with their weaknesses and so are more disposed to pay attention to the formative process the candidates are going through. They are not so needy of love or control. At least, they are aware of their needs and do their best to control themselves. When they fail, they do not hesitate to apologize. They genuinely love and care for the candidates and not because they need their love in return. At the same time, they do not compromise the values of the Christian vocation. Hence, they are authoritative and empowering of the candidates.

Implications

The formation styles I have tried to classify in this chapter are meant to show how the personality needs of formators could affect positively or negatively the formation of the candidates to the priesthood and the consecrated life. There is no denying the fact that formators have more impact by their personality than by what they say, no matter how intelligent what they say appear or sound. What is being advocated for is not that perfect formators must be found for the formation houses. None actually exists. Rather, it is an invitation to formators to learn to listen to themselves, evaluate themselves and their actions, motivations and their feelings towards the candidates and towards formation itself. These points that I am making presuppose that the formators actually are happy working in formation houses. If they do not like the formation apostolate, it will be useless to send them there.

Chapter Five

Stages of Formation: Goals and Indications

My objective in this chapter is to examine the goals and indications of formation at different stages of formation in the light of the ideals or values of the African culture. Again, the contents are simply general outlines from which particular Institutes should feel free to make their own adaptation. In 2005 the Catholic Bishops Conference of Nigeria (CBCN) published the *Ratio Fundamentalis Institutionis Sacerdotalis* for the formation of priests in Nigeria. The content of that document is relevant for the formation of priests in Africa. It will be my guide in my reflections for the formation of diocesan priests.

Forming Candidates for the Diocesan Priesthood

Minor Seminary

In *Ratio Fundamentalis Institutionis Sacerdotalis*, the Bishops of Nigeria describe minor seminary as "a seminarium, that is, seed bed where the foundation of Christian life is laid in a very solid form so that seminarians may grow with healthy spiritual, social and moral life ...." (CBCN, 2005, n. 31) The minor seminary occupies a significant place in the project of integral human development of future priests because the young boys are still tender in the sense that the structures of their personality are still malleable to formation. This is the time in which foundation is laid for the formation of solid moral and religious character. The appreciation of the central position of the minor seminaries in the formation of future priests should be evident in the context of the words of the fathers of the 1990 Synod on the formation of priests, which John Paul II quoted verbatim in *Pastores Dabo Vobis*, that "the whole work of priestly formation would be deprived of its necessary foundation if it lacked a suitable human formation" (n. 43; Proposition 21). Minor seminary therefore is a period of serious tilling of the soil of humanity of the future candidates for the priesthood. It should be taken to be an opportune period that should be exploited fully.

Development of moral conscience is of great importance at this stage of development. The *Ratio* notes that our society has largely lost the strong moral sense of what is wrong and what is right (CBCN, 2005, n. 5). Conscience is an important aspect of authentic personal identity, and is the basis for the construction of authentic religious identity (Vergote, 1999). This aspect of personal development is most challenging in many African countries today because moral norms seem to be blatantly rejected. This condition has reached a discouraging level in some countries than in others. Children who come into the minor seminary are from families with various deficiencies in the formation of their conscience, in addition to the confusion they experience from the world around them. The minor seminary becomes a period of helping these children change some of malformation that has taken place in their conscience. This learning comes more by imitation and modeling than from too much talking. This is true at all levels of our formation, but more at the minor seminary. This calls for transparency and a sense of moral conviction in the lives of formators and in their dealings with the seminarians.

Secondly, formators of minor seminarians should be attuned to the developmental age and tasks of the children in the minor seminaries. These children, though seminarians, are still children. They are not priests. Though they desire to be priests, their desire is not yet fine-tuned or processed in a personal manner. Their desire is still largely a result of admiration for priests or the desires of their parents or uncles or aunts. Yet, it is from these desires that the genuine and personalized desire grows. That is why it is a delicate period of formation. This means that minor seminarians, especially those in junior secondary level, should not be told constantly that they should start early to live like priests because they take this suggestion as an imperative. When they go home, the parents and their communities call them "little priests". From Junior Secondary School, these children are already marked out and treated like priests in school and at home. For this same reason, the developmental difficulties and challenges of pre-pubescent and pubescent stages are often not identified and consciously followed in the seminary. Seminarians are left to themselves to understand and manage the problems of that period of their life. In other words, they are expected to live like mature adults who should be able to handle most of their problems. If it is suggested to them to feel that they are already priests and should not make mistakes, they learn to hide their mistakes and to be too secretive and fearful. Secondly, they can develop an exaggerated sense of guilt over minor mistakes. The fear of expressing their deepest problems to the authorities and the spying stance of their home communities make the situation very difficult for many of them. By the time they finish minor seminary, some of them have learned so well the art of hiding, secretiveness, lying and other tricks to protect themselves and their goal to become priest with the psychological hang-ups that go with that. Children should be allowed to be children. They should be permitted to make their own mistakes and be led to learn the lessons from their mistakes. In the Decree on the Training of Priests, *Optatam Totius*, the fathers of the Second Vatican Council insist that minor seminarians "are to lead a life suitable to the age, maturity and development of young people, in keeping with the principles of sound psychology. Nor should they be deprived of social contact with their families" (OT, n. 3).

The task of identity formation at adolescence is made more complex by the upsurge of sexual hormones during this stage of development. In many cases, students are not told anything directly about their sexual and gender identity at this period. Rather, emphasis is placed on avoiding sexual intercourse due to future life of celibacy. Fearing to speak to someone about these feelings, the adolescent turns to his peers who may advise him to masturbate and/or engage in mutual masturbation. This is the time some adolescents may be introduced to pornography and different forms of sexualized play with both men and women. It is from this period that many sexual addictions are learned which become difficult to give up in the future (Coleman, 2002). Their vulnerable condition can easily be exploited by immature adults who are also fixated at this stage of development.

Finally, though minor seminarians are children, formators should try to address them with respect. Children learn to respect themselves when they feel respected. Sometimes, even those in Senior Secondary School are treated and spoken to as if they are babies or slaves. Respect should not be commanded; it has to be earned by one respecting oneself. It is a necessary aspect of authentic self-esteem that persons have a strong sense of self-respect. This self-perception is the condition for a more disinterested assessment of facts in adulthood. When people are treated without genuine respect, they tend to learn the art of slavish conformity, which makes an adult to behave sometimes like an unthinking idiot. We notice this in certain attitudes of some ordained priests and the surprising reasoning they put forward to justify those attitudes. In some other persons being treated without genuine respect results in rebelliousness. When such get into leadership positions, they tend to become authoritarian in their style.

Transition to Spiritual Year: Selection of Candidates

Since all the candidates for the priesthood do not come from the minor seminaries, the *Ratio* provides space for the orientation of candidates from the minor seminaries and those who are not from the minor seminaries. These two categories of seminarians are considered in transition to the spiritual year (CBCN, 2005, n. 38). Let me say that the conscious journey to the diocesan priesthood starts with the selection of the candidates for the spiritual year. In other words, it should be taken for granted that a person who offers himself to be considered for the spiritual year has personally thought about and desired to become a priest. This inner disposition is necessary for genuine discernment.

Because of the importance of the spiritual year in the current training of diocesan priests in some parts of Africa today, it is of utmost importance to select candidates very carefully (CBCN, 2005, n. 79). This selection should be carried out by competent persons, and psychological assessment of the candidates should be done by competent psychologists who follow psychological theories that agree with Christian anthropology. Proper psychological assessment should be able to describe the psychological pillars upon which a person's humanity is founded. Such an assessment helps to make selection process very decisive (OT, n.6). It is unfortunate that many dioceses in Africa are still reluctant to make use of the tools of psychology in this initial selection. Almost every institute of consecrated life in Africa today, male and female, is doing its best to see that professional psychological assessment constitutes an integral part of its understanding of their candidates and in their selection process. The dioceses are still lagging behind in this important aspect of the selection process and it is a big lack. Moreover, dioceses have professionals in various fields of study but do not seem to have enough trained personnel in this area.

On this note, it seems very important that candidates who willingly desire to proceed to the priesthood after their Secondary School or High School (that is, after their minor seminary) should make official application to the rector of their spiritual year seminaries. This application is meant to indicate that the seminarian in question willingly desires to continue with the formation to the priesthood and that he is taking responsibility for the decision. This practice will initiate in some candidates the process of owning the choice of the priesthood especially for those who found themselves in the minor seminary because their parents decided to send them there. Moreover, the application should mark for the seminarian a decisive turning point in his desire to be a priest. That moment of decision is critical for the young adult to make. The rector of the spiritual year will now discuss with his bishop the number of applications and then decide, according to the directives of the diocese, the necessary steps to take in the selection. One cannot emphasize enough the importance of this initial decision and selection in the formation of the future priests.

The implication of this proposal then is that minor seminary should no longer serve as a direct road to the major seminary. The direct link between minor and major seminary makes it so difficult for some minor seminarians to decide whether to continue for the priesthood or not. If the direct link between minor seminary and major seminary is removed, it will spare the seminarians the social stereotyping as already-made priests, which does not allow them to be themselves and to live out the dynamics, difficulties, and challenges of their specific age of development. But if after thinking through their experiences and desires, they feel the priesthood is their vocation, they can now apply in writing to the diocese of their choice. This, I believe strongly, will have a lot of positive effect on the formation in the spiritual year.

Spiritual Year

It is interesting that the Bishops of Nigeria in the *Ratio* find a similarity between the spiritual year and the novitiates of the Institutes of Consecrated Life (CBCN, 2005, n. 41). The novitiate is the time that institutes of consecrated life introduce their candidates to their style of life in an intense and intentional way. It is the period the candidates are concretely helped to assimilate the values and charism of their institutes. Hence, it is considered the period of initial formation. In the same manner, the spiritual year should be a time that candidates for the diocesan priesthood are consciously introduced into the meaning, values, and lifestyle of diocesan priests, and are also helped to assimilate them to a reasonable extent before they get into philosophical studies. For this reason, the *Ratio* calls the spiritual year a "period of initiation into the spiritual journey of the priest"(CBCN, 2005, n. 44). The formative relevance of the spiritual year emerges within this framework: it should be the intense transitional year during which the future diocesan priest is concretely exposed to the experience of priesthood as essentially a spiritual calling, and is challenged in all that he is and has to open himself and internalize the values, meaning, and attitudes expressed in the diocesan priesthood. It is a year in which the future priest gives focused attention to the priestly life as an integral aspect of his self-ideal.

In concrete, this means that the spiritual year should be a year of spiritual awakening of the candidates to the inner life of the priest. Most importantly, it is the period during which the candidates are exposed to a deepened experience of God in a personal manner so that they can develop a personal relationship with Him; through this experience they grow in making their own the religious identity already received at baptism but which has now to constitute a significant part of their self-definition. In this sense, a valid experience of God must touch all the components of the psyche: the mind, heart and will. It is more than an intellectual reflection on the scripture. This spiritual awakening naturally leads them to meditation and contemplative prayer, which they must appreciate if they are to live a fulfilled and joyful priestly life. A diocesan priest must be a contemplative; otherwise, he will find it extremely difficult to tune in to the center of his life in the midst of active apostolate (Nouwen, 1989). While the liturgy of the hours is important as a prayer of the Church, effort should be made to help candidates establish solid patterns of personal prayer, and private time with the Lord. As diocesan priests, they will not always be praying the liturgy of the hours as in the communities of the institutes of consecrated life. If the personal relationship with the Lord is not very important to them, they will not be able to pray the breviary when they are by themselves, alone or when they go through the hectic activities that fill their day (CBCN, 2005, n. 48). During the holidays, some seminarians forget their breviaries in the seminary chapel, and some neatly pack it in their suitcases in their rooms, and simply go home. This indicates that they do not see the value outside the normal school timetable. There are some priests who pray it as a burdensome duty. For example, there are priests who pray all the hours at night to make sure nothing bothers them the following day. How do such priests understand their relationship with God and prayer?

Spiritual year is an intense period to develop what Aschenbrenner (2002) describes as "monasticism of the heart", which is the core of the diocesan priest's spirituality. Monasticism of the heart expresses that radical solitude which the diocesan priest lives with God even in the midst of the demanding apostolate. The foundation of it is a profound experience of God in which God's love becomes so strong in a person's motivational system as to effect a powerful shift in the center of gravity that holds his life. In this experienced love, everything is relativized and God and the values of the Gospel become the hub of the candidate's life. This is the core of the priesthood as a spiritual calling (Synod of Bishops, 1990), and candidates are introduced into this reality in the spiritual year. Secondly, it is growth in this love that provides the valid psychological reason and the energy to live a life of renunciation. It is in line with this that Ronco (1994) emphasizes that "the initial formation in chastity is not avoiding sin, but growing in personal love for Christ"(p. 165).

Spiritual awakening should be accompanied with clarification of values, such as the Gospel counsels of obedience, chastity and poverty (CBCN, 2005, n. 48). This has to happen at both the theoretical and the concrete and individual levels. The following guidelines are suggested:

- First, the candidates should be presented with these values in a clear manner and be helped to see the variety of their interpretations and implications in the world around them. Concrete examples deriving from culture and their surroundings are important here.

- After that, each person should be challenged to explore how these values are present in him, and how they experience the tension between these values and the values of the gospel which the priestly life embodies. This is a very concrete way of knowing the strength of certain needs in the candidates and the extent they can permit themselves to be confronted with the values of the Gospel. Moreover, this exercise helps them to purify their intention in a conscious manner.

- Frequent (weekly or biweekly) colloquy with each candidate during this period should aim at helping the candidates know themselves more and to see the relevant areas they need to grow and the areas they experience deeper difficulty. Here, effort should be made to verify the kind of conflicts a candidate feels towards certain cultural values in the light of the priestly values.

- The candidates should be helped to see how personally held values are related to social order or disorder. This is a very important exercise that should open the eyes of the candidates to begin to see the connection between structures of injustice in the world and the structures present in concrete human beings.

Spiritual year is also the time that the affectivity of the seminarians is closely assessed and nurtured. Affectivity is the very big issue in our lives, and for persons being trained in celibate living, maturity in this area is of tremendous importance. A seminarian's affective capacity should be considered within his developmental history. Proper psychological assessment should be able to describe a person's relational beliefs, attitudes and tendencies. During the spiritual year, workshops should be organized on affectivity. These workshops should dwell on the theoretical views about human nature, since our beliefs about affectivity derive from our views of human nature. The dualism of body and spirit, and the degradation of the body and sexuality, are no longer accepted by the teaching authority of the Church (DCE, 2005, pt. 1). Appreciation of the unity of the human being will lead to appreciating the need to grow in one's humanity as body and spirit. Questions of relationship and the perturbations present in relationships should be openly discussed, and the students challenged to examine the different strategies they adopt in dealing with affective matters such as avoidance of relationship, erotic relationships, compulsive masturbation, and mature relationships where there is respect, openness and appropriate maintenance of boundaries. Attention should also be given to sexual preoccupations of seminarians and their contents. Workshops should be able to explore in detail these issues. Secondly, the important issues of sexual identity and sexual orientation should also be a significant aspect of this workshop package on affectivity, as well as the variety of sexual deviation and sexual crimes. The degree of affective maturity is a very important factor in living a healthy and joyful celibate life (CBCN, 2005, n. 26).

The spiritual year, therefore, is the first decisive time when the integral maturity of the candidates is assessed. Having accompanied them intensely for one year, the formators should be able to know the candidates reasonably enough to note the strong *pillars* upon which their personalities are constructed, their *basic needs* especially those that are central in their psychological world, their *affective beliefs and capacities*, and the extent the *ideals* of the priesthood have been assimilated into their motivational system as that for which they want to dedicate their lives (n. 44). Unless the ideals of the priesthood constitute the center of their motivation, and the driving force of their thoughts, emotions, and actions, the future priests may not find real meaning and happiness in their lives as priests.

All this implies then that the spiritual year should not be converted into a college or a mini-philosophicum. Unfortunately, so many subjects are taught in some spiritual year seminaries. Again, the tendency to turn everything into academics is prevalent in the formation of diocesan priests. The *Ratio*, for example, outlines 13 courses to be taught in the spiritual year. Yet, it is a period in which the candidates should be assisted to acquire spiritual disciplines such as the art of meditation, journaling, spiritual direction, and spiritual reading, which will help them develop this monasticism of the heart that they need to function well as diocesan priests. Effort should be made to reduce academic courses to be taught to the barest minimum since they will have a lot of time to study some of these subjects when they get into philosophy and theology. At the end of the Spiritual Year period, candidates should have become more aware of their strengths and weaknesses, and the areas of their personalities that need greater conversion to Jesus Christ, whom they have grown to know and to love personally. Secondly, the ideals of the priestly life should constitute a significant aspect of their self-definition. This initial identification with the priestly life and values provides them the psychological base necessary to go into serious intellectual formation in the philosophicum.

Philosophical Studies

Philosophical studies provide the future priests the tools necessary for critical thinking and a deeper understanding of the human condition and the questions that plague human existence. During this period, they are then presented with the various philosophical theories that have been developed by philosophers to explain the world, the place of human beings in it, and the destiny of the universe. They are challenged to examine these theories critically and draw out their implications in the face of the ultimate questions of life.

Students should be helped to know that all philosophical reflection arises from concrete situations and contexts. That is why the *Ratio* lays emphasis on African philosophy (CBCN, 2005, n. 52). Philosophical thoughts are not mere speculations outside the ordinary life of human beings. As students are guided through the history of philosophy and the perennial problems, they should be challenged to draw out for themselves why these studies are necessary for them as human beings and as future priests. Secondly, they should be helped to see the relationship between classroom philosophy and the concrete life they live outside. It is unfortunate that our seminarians believe that philosophy is merely about arguments and counter arguments, speaking in obtuse language, or dismissing everything simply with a wave of the hand. Some believe that these are the defining qualities of philosophers. A seminarian was so happy that no one was able to understand what he wrote. I questioned him about it and he said that it was a good sign that he actually learned the philosophy he was taught. If he were to be comprehensible, he would have cheapened himself as a student of philosophy. This is nothing but arrogance and a demonstration of emptiness. Such a distorted idea of philosophy should be discouraged. Oftentimes, it is promoted by superficial knowledge of philosophers and their ideas.

The condition of Africa poses a serious challenge to our philosophical studies. If the philosophical studies in the seminaries are to redefine and remodel African thought and vision for the better (CBCN, 2005, n. 53, vi), then philosophy teachers have an enormous task before them. As much as possible, the lectures have to be able to guide the seminarians through seasoned philosophical reasoning on concrete situations and vice versa. In this manner, students learn to understand and explain issues from theory to concrete situation and from concrete situations to the level of theory. Inability to make this back and forth movement between theory and concrete life-situations is a big lack in the intellectual formation of our seminarians. First of all, it indicates a limitation in their creative or imaginative ability (CBCN, 2005, n. 55), that is, the ability to broaden their horizon so as to understand an issue from a larger perspective. Secondly, this lack makes it hard for them to deal with different points of view, especially in our multi-ethnic continent and increasingly pluralistic world today. It generally tends to make them hold onto their position or that of their group without the ability to justify it persuasively. In fact, some African priests in the United States are thrown out of rectories and are prohibited from celebrating Mass, not merely out of racism but because of their inability to deal reasonably and intellectually with the conflicting perspectives in the American culture and Church. Fighting, raising of voice, and stamping one's feet for emphasis do not indicate a well-reasoned argument for one's position. Priests often get away with it in many parts of Africa where the Church is still largely "Father's Church". In the West and North America, they may not get away with it.

Another significant aspect of philosophical studies is that they should be able to lead the seminarians towards greater conviction in their beliefs and about their priestly identity which they have acquired during the spiritual year. The various deep questions about humanity which philosophy raises should be able to arouse their own questions about themselves and the world around them. In addition, they have also to deal with other questions that are more personal, such as their affective needs. For the seminarians who are open to these questions, it could lead them to serious crisis of vocational identity and meaning. This crisis is very necessary for them to question themselves and thus think through their own beliefs and identity, and then arrive at a more personalized understanding of who they want to be. This is a very critical time for many of them because some do misinterpret this condition as lack of vocation. They need special attention at this time. They should be free to discuss this matter with their spiritual directors and/counselors. Spiritual directors should also be able to understand what is happening to the students and guide them appropriately. At the same time, attention should also be paid to those seminarians who avoid all forms of questions and doubts, because they believe it is against their faith. If nothing is done, this group of seminarians often turn out closed up intellectually to serious questions and perspectives about certain issues. The faith they hold has not been digested, and they do not want to go through the pains of personal understanding of their faith. Such seminarians appear to have infantile and defensive identification with the institutional church to the point of fusion, where their sense of self is totally lost.

Through the experience of crisis of vocational identity at this period, the identity acquired during the spiritual year is shaken, de-structured and re-structured. At the end of the philosophical studies, the student should be able to be more at peace in and with himself, that he is making the right decision and that the priesthood is a worthy call to respond to with all his life. This, in my opinion, should be the inner disposition with which a seminarian should proceed to theological studies.

Theological Studies

Theology is more than a rational reflection on the objective truths of the Christian faith. Such limited understanding of theology oftentimes leads to a mere intellectual assent to a set of propositions clearly evidenced as truth. Theological studies should be more than knowing intellectually the teachings of the Church in the same manner that one knows the truths of mathematics. Such knowing, though an affirmation of the objectivity of the truth of faith, can remain just as impersonal as the knowledge that seven plus five equals twelve. The Christian faith is first of all based on truth embodied in our Lord Jesus Christ and this truth is accessed through relationship with Him. This truth is therefore grounded in trust in the activities of God in human history (the economy of salvation) and in the lives of individuals. The articulation of these truth in theological discourses is therefore a second step.

The task, therefore, of theological formation of candidates for the Catholic priesthood is primarily the personal appropriation of the truths of the Christian faith. This means, making one's own (from the Latin *proprius*) the truth of Christianity. In this manner, the objective truths of our faith are supposed to be handles for opening the door to the mystery of what God has revealed of Himself and leading the candidates to establish and nurture a relationship between them and a personal God, the

Father of Our Lord Jesus Christ in the bosom of the Church, the Bride and the mystical Body of Christ.

What is at stake here is the fact that a priest is fundamentally a religious person, someone for whom God is alive; someone in whose heart a continuous dialogue with the Trinitarian God takes place in a conscious manner. In other words, the truths of our faith do not simply belong to the intellect; they do, but they must effect radical changes in the heart of men and women. It is this point that Henri Nouwen (1989) makes when he states that in the end what matters is whether God is alive in the hearts of priests. So theology cannot stay "in the head"; it has to move to the heart. Theology is a prayerful activity and not primarily an intellectual one!

Unless theological formation of the priests enables the objective truth of our faith to become the truth that *they are*, that is, appropriated, that formation has not really succeeded. Appropriation does not happen once and for all; it is an ongoing process. Appropriation requires further appropriation in the face of new questions, new challenges and new changes in the world and in the life of individual priests. Unappropriated theological knowledge only forms the intellect, which might be swollen with pride on account of its knowledge of theological propositions. It becomes tragic when such a theological egghead is animated by a heart that is shriveled up for lack of faith and love of God. Barrette (1958) makes this clear: "A learned theologian may be in possession of all the so-called truths of rational theology, able to prove and disprove propositions and generally hold his own dialectically with the best; and yet in his heart God may have died or never lived. On the other hand, an illiterate peasant who knows nothing of formal theology, who may not even be able to state accurately the tenets of his creed, nevertheless may succeed in *being* religious. He is in the truth, ... and people who

107

know him can recognize this fact from his presence, his bearing, his way of life"(p. 171).

Theologians in the seminaries and houses of formation should do their best to teach with deep conviction. It often happens that the formators' lack of conviction or even skepticism is more easily communicated to the candidates than their erudition. As young men in the first half of their lives, most of these candidates may find their role models in these formator-theologians who are even in doubt of what they teach. Some of the theology lecturers teach only because they have to and not because they have any real personal approach to it. This impersonal relationship with the truths of the Christian faith does not seem to be effective in the formation of priests. In the light of this Häring (1989) clearly states that the starting point for any reformation of the Catholic priesthood "must always be our collaborative efforts at wholly knowing Christ the Healer, Prophet, and the Incarnated image of the Creator"(p. 22). He emphasizes the need for theology to help priests become mirror images, living symbols, of Jesus Christ. Such is possible when theology is approached not as a cerebral subject but as an encounter with the person of Jesus Christ and all that He stands for in the history of humanity.

Continuity and Structural Issues in the Formation of Diocesan Priests

Necessity for Continuity in Formation Stages

From the start, it is necessary to state the importance of continuity in formation of priests and the religious men and women. This is seriously lacking in the formation of diocesan priests in some parts of the African continent. At least, I know that in Nigeria, this continuity is seriously lacking. Each stage of formation appears to be unique and unrelated to others except merely as stages one has to pass through to become a priest. For instance, when seminarians are sent to the major seminaries from the spiritual year, the formators have to start from the beginning to know them. Yet, these persons have spent one year of spiritual experience. The same happens when they are sent to theology. It always feels like a new start with new students. For this reason, there is little, if any, coordination among the formators at different stages of formation. Those in spiritual year do their own business and pass over seminarians to the formators of the philosophy faculty. At the end of philosophical studies, these students are simply passed over to the formators in theology. The only link is the Bishop who actually sends the seminarian to another stage or withdraws him.

This lack of coordination and collaboration makes formation more tedious when the number of seminarians is large. What happens is that formators do their best to know the seminarians, but succeed, in most cases, in knowing their external behaviours. This is reflected in the reports which often are based on attendance to chapel, function, class performance, silence, and other good manners. These are good indicators of behaviour and help in judgment, but they could be very deceptive. Clever persons can fake all these perfectly well and get into the priesthood with their ambiguous intentions. This situation is not really fair either to the seminarians or to the formators. The formators can only do so much with what they have; and seminarians can only grow within the possibilities provided to them.

The formation of religious men and women is generally continuous. They move from being aspirants to being postulants, to the novitiate, to philosophical and theological studies, and to ordination or profession. Throughout these stages, their formators grow in their knowledge of the candidates, and are in better situation to give appropriate help to each of them. Religious congregations usually transfer the files of their candidates to the next stage in formation. But in the formation of diocesan priests, each stage is so discontinuous with the previous ones that formators at each stage have to start all over to learn to know the candidates. By the time they are coming to know who the candidates are, they are moved to the next stage.

Secondly, there is little continuity between the life in the seminary and the life diocesan priests live after ordination. We do everything in common in the seminary, while after ordination the diocesan priest is left to himself to manage his time and freedom. This lack of continuity makes some priests feel like fish out of water. Some feel unable to manage themselves in their new freedom. And so, some get themselves into certain troubles and pursue illegitimate ambitions they set for themselves. Religious men and women, on the other hand, more often experience continuity between their formation and the life they live after ordination or profession. From the very start, they live in communities and are trained to develop community spirit. The experience of community living from the beginning of their formation and through the years of professed or ordained life provides religious men and women the constant challenge to imbibe the spirit of community. As difficult as it may be sometimes to some of them, at least, it is not foreign or new to their style of life.

Restructuring the Formational Situation of Diocesan Priests

For the reasons advanced in the preceding section, I feel that the structures put in place in our seminaries and the model of seminary formation are still largely good for the formation of members of the institutes for consecrated life and not for the formation of diocesan priests. Religious priests, classified as monastic and apostolic, live in communities and have mobility as their basic characteristic (Rausch, 1990). A diocesan priest is basically a pastor in charge of a marked out portion of the people of God. He exercises his priesthood among this people. For this reason, he is more prone to be alone than his religious counterparts who enjoy the support of their religious community. Without a strong spiritual base, the diocesan priest risks losing his bearing in the pastoral activities that call his attention daily. For this reason, the newly ordained priests in a research in the United States strongly emphasize that diocesan seminarians should cultivate a strong prayer life in the seminary. No one doubts the importance of this in the training of diocesan priests. The major question is: How can this spiritual base be cultivated if the model of forming diocesan priests largely follows that of the semi-monastic model obtained in the pre-Vatican II period? It is in the light of this observation that I believe that the current structures put in place for the formation of the diocesan priests in our seminaries should be reviewed.

Restructuring the Spiritual Year

Since the spiritual year marks the concrete and conscious starting point for the training of diocesan priests a lot of energy and resources should be invested there. It is the place where seminarians are introduced to a deep and personal experience of the God they had encountered in the sacraments of baptism, confirmation, reconciliation, and the daily Eucharist. Love of this God should be seen and experienced strongly enough for the young man to feel invited to give himself totally to it. For this reason, the spiritual year should be really a year of *spiritual experience and discipline.*

- The number of courses taught in the spiritual year should be reduced to a minimum. For instance, the *Ratio* produced by the Catholic Bishops Conference of Nigeria (n. 50) stipulates 13 courses. That is too many if we want to give the seminarians the time they need to develop the discipline of personal reflection and personal relationship with God, which is the fundamental objective of the spiritual year (CBCN, 2005, n. 42). Courses like Church Music, Communication Skills, The Art of Liturgical Reading, Liturgy, English and Latin, could be removed. These could be done in the first year philosophy, if need be. Human sexuality and priestly celibacy could be treated under Human Development. As much as possible, the courses should be taught in a very personal and interactive manner that should challenge their lives and their ability for personal reflection. If exams should be done, emphasis should be placed on personal understanding of materials taught rather than mechanical reproduction of what has been memorized. Internalization of the values of the priesthood is a primary goal here, and so, memorization of materials does not help at all in achieving this goal.

- The year should be a time to teach them what the priesthood means. This should be taught in a way that makes the priesthood attractive to them. There are some who are attracted to the priesthood for very external reasons such as cars, comfort, education, financial security, and the popularity of prayer ministry. They should be helped to see the danger of getting into the priesthood for these reasons. Young men want to dedicate their lives to something meaningful, and the service of the Gospel in the priesthood is such a great project of life if they feel called to it. Secondly, this is the time to teach them the charism of the diocesan priesthood as different from those of priests of religious congregations. They should know from the very start that diocesan priests are first and foremost pastors who work with and for the people of God. They are not called to become professors, research fellows, international speakers, and so on. If they happen to be any of these (and sometimes they are, for example, professors teaching in the seminary) it is secondary to their basic vocation and charism. This is important for them to know because there is growing confusion about the meaning of diocesan priesthood among diocesan priests today. The craze for further study for its own sake that has been present among them is destroying the heart of diocesan priesthood.

- It is also important that spiritual year seminarians should choose the appropriate time in the day that is suitable to do their meditation. It should be a time they hope to maintain. They should also be able to explain why that time is conducive for them. Suppose a particular time is not suitable for the school as a whole, the seminarian should be encouraged to look for another time. This manner of approach is necessary because in the normal parish setting, a diocesan priest should be able to be flexible to the demands of the apostolate, while still maintaining his time with the Lord.

- In this connection, Liturgy of the Hours could be said in the choir for the first five months of the spiritual year. After that, it could be reduced to Sundays and perhaps other three days of the week. The remaining days, seminarians should be encouraged to pray it on their own. The whole training here should be on responsible freedom (CBCN, 2005, n. 46), which is the fruit of personalized formation.

- Since this one year is a year of spiritual experience, it may be good to reduce the number of holidays given to spiritual year seminarians. I am inclined to the view that they do not go on holidays at all. This suggestion may be resisted but if we realize that the priesthood is to a certain degree a liminal life, a whole year of spiritual experience makes the seminarians realize the decisiveness of the step they are taking towards the priesthood. Going on holidays often makes them feel that they are simply going through the same process as in the minor seminary. Some seminarians feel that they are simply moving from one stage to the other without giving personal thought to what they are getting into, only to see themselves, suddenly, approaching the priesthood.

- Having said all this, it means that the spiritual year seminaries need resources to provide the seminarians the kind of formation that should be foundational to their future life as priests. If it is truly accepted that the spiritual year occupies an important foundational place in the formation of the diocesan priests, then the formation team should not be left to spend their time looking for funds to manage the seminary. Dioceses should provide enough resources for their formation. This implies that the seminaries should take only the number of seminarians they can give a proper training to. This is a sensitive matter because some people feel that young persons who feel called to the priesthood should be allowed to follow their desires. While this is the ideal, it is important to emphasize that these desires are also limited by particular circumstances. It will be unfair, both to the candidates and the formators, to try to train twenty people, for example, with resources that will be adequate for only ten people in the name of giving a chance to all who desire to become priests. It is significant to remember that men are CALLED to the priesthood by God in, through and for the ecclesial community. It is about God and this ecclesial community and not a matter of satisfying the desires of the candidates however genuine and noble these are. This is another way of saying that no one has a right to priesthood.

• Finally, all that has been said so far goes to show that formators, especially those in spiritual year seminaries, should be properly trained in the field of formation. They should be knowledgeable in psycho-spirituality and the teachings of the Church (CBCN, 2005, n. 80). Also, they should have been accompanied in their own growth so that they do not confuse their own personal problems with that of the seminarians. The persons being trained for this work should show interest in it. Let me repeat what has been said above: no one should be compelled to engage in the delicate apostolate of forming others for the priesthood or religious life. Expertise is necessary for the integral formation that today's seminarians need. To be involved in the formation process should presume expertise and a willingness to offer this expertise to the service of the Church in the formation of others.

Revisiting the Structures of the Major Seminary

Major seminaries on the continent are owned by groups of dioceses. Since these dioceses send their seminarians to these major seminaries after the spiritual year formation, it is important that the spiritual year seminaries have the same program. The is not about uniformity but to ensure that the seminarians in the major seminary have comparably similar experiences and hopefully have personalized the decision become priests. Some spiritual year programs are merely a continuation of the secondary school program. Some do not have any program at all. This makes the seminarians see it as just an obligatory stage to pass through in order to get to the major seminary. Such thinking destroys the objective of the spiritual year. From time to time, it is important that the formation staff of the spiritual year seminaries meet to review the program they follow. At the end of every spiritual year, detailed reports on the selected seminarians for philosophical studies should be written. These reports should include a person's strength, gifts, and weaknesses, and areas to pay special attention to. Each report should have two copies, one for the bishop and one for the seminary to which the seminarian is sent for philosophical studies.

At the beginning of each academic year, the formators in the philosophy stage should be able to read through all these reports of the new students in order to know how to guide them. Spiritual directors should also get the reports of the seminarians assigned to them. Because of the large number in some seminaries, seminarians have been divided into houses with a house moderator. This means that each house moderator should read closely the reports of those seminarians under him so as to give them the necessary guidance they need. The essence is to know them well in order to assist them in their growth. The large number of seminarians is a blessing, but can also constitute a serious obstacle to formation. One big disadvantage of large number is that formation oftentimes focuses on control of seminarians and maintenance of order and discipline (Schineller, 2001). The individual is often lost in the crowd. In order to check this excessive loss of the uniqueness of individual seminarians, the housing strategy should be taken very seriously, more than just having house Masses once a week, as is practiced in some seminaries. Sometimes, it will be good for the houses to pray the liturgy of the hours together on certain days of the week. Some seminaries are doing that already. The Jesuit priest, Fr. Dom Totaro (2005) has come up with a model of spiritual exercises designed for small group of persons without a director. Such a model of spiritual formation is incredibly valuable for diocesan priests, especially where the number of seminarians is large. He has already tried this in some seminaries with great results.

What has been presented here shows that formators in the major seminaries are much more than lecturers who simply teach their courses and do other businesses that concern them. As formators, they are guides to the seminarians and they should give them appropriate and loving attention. If these processes are followed well, formators will notice that their assessment of students at the end of each year will not be overly tedious. They shall have been able to know the students in such a way as to make good vocational judgment about them.

The formation of the diocesan priest is much more training in the acquisition of responsible freedom, that is, the ability for the future priest to manage his life responsibly without anyone having to watch him. Seminarians who must be told everything before they do it are not showing good sign of this responsibility. Seminary formators should take it seriously. This is where functions or charges given to seminarians are an important aspect of checking how creative and responsible a person can be even when he is not being watched. This is not training in conformity; it is letting the future priests take responsibility for their lives and their decisions. This sense of responsibility should start in a deeply conscious way in the spiritual year.

There need to be structures by which formators meet, coordinate their activities, support each other, are "supervised" either by the person in charge of formation or in a "peer supervision" model, and so on.

In order to achieve these objectives it is also important for each seminary to have what we call formation personnel. These persons are those well-trained in the art and dynamics of formation, just like the Rectors of spiritual year seminaries (CBCN, 2005, n. 80). Due to their training, they have keener perception of the inner workings of a formative environment and how the individuals respond to formative interventions. These people can reduce the enormous work-load of the Rector who is the overall administrator of the seminary. In the current formation model in our seminaries, the Rector is both the administrator and the formation person, with the Vice Rector and Administrative Dean being basically concerned with maintenance of order and discipline. A formation team in a major seminary includes all those involved in the formation of the candidates. This team could be said to comprise the four arms indicated in the chart below.

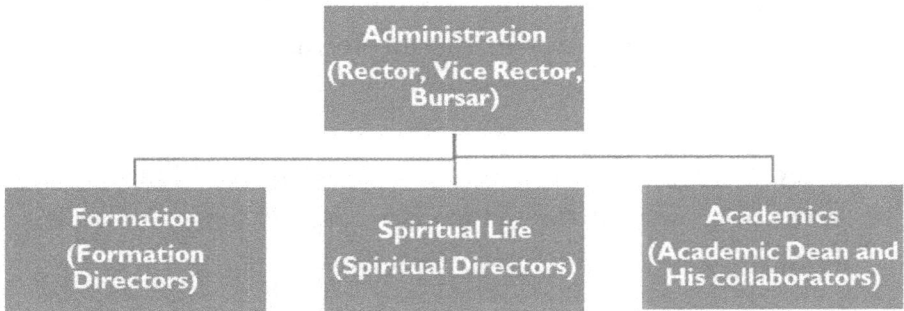

```
┌────────────────────────────┐
│      Administration         │
│  (Rector, Vice Rector,      │
│         Bursar)             │
└────────────────────────────┘
```

| Formation (Formation Directors) | Spiritual Life (Spiritual Directors) | Academics (Academic Dean and His collaborators) |

- The *Administrative arm* consists of the Rector, the Vice Rector, the Bursar, and the various councils that the administration works with. This arm is the unifying arm of the formation team, that is, all the formators. The major concern of this arm is the business of the seminary as an institution, coordinating different aspects of it while focusing on the overall goal of the seminary.
- The *Formation arm* occupies a very significant place in this scheme. The members should be well-trained in the art and dynamics of formation. The formators in this arm know the candidates personally and follow them in their journey. Their work is beyond maintaining order and discipline; it is largely understanding the candidates and challenging their growth process. They are specialized in the human formation of the candidates. The Administrative Arm relies heavily on this arm for proper discernment of vocations. By

their training, they should be able to know the students very well and be present to them. They belong to the external forum. This is what differentiates them from the spiritual directors.

• The *Academic arm* comprises the Academic Dean and his collaborators, and sees to the intellectual formation of the seminarians.

• The *Spiritual Life arm* comprises the spiritual directors. They belong to the internal forum. This arm follows the spiritual growth of the seminarians, the challenges they face in their personal relationship with God.

If these four arms are clearly defined and the personnel of each of them well-trained, we shall be able to give the seminarians the kind of formation they need. It does not promise a perfect outcome, but just what human beings could do on their own part, and God will surely bless the efforts.

Formation of Candidates for the Consecrated Life

Postulancy

In some institutes of consecrated life, the period of postulancy comes after the time of aspirancy or *experience* as some Institutes call it. The names do not really matter. What is most important is that postulancy is the period that precedes entrance into the novitiate. Both entail involvement with the life of the religious congregation but the involvement is less intense during postulancy.

This period, in my opinion, is very important in the discernment of vocations. The goal of this stage of formation is to examine the candidate's reasons for applying to the institute. It is also the period during which they are introduced into the general themes and values of the consecrated life and their specific incarnation in the Institute, to see if they are truly open to it.

Now, this is a critical time when the values of the culture should be presented to these candidates in clear terms and how the consecrated life, expressed in the style of life of the institute, could create certain tension in them. It is not enough for the candidates at this stage to be able to answer all the catechism questions well or be effusive in their pious expressions. Some come in too young and some enter after getting their degrees or diplomas. The presentation of the cultural implications of the life they feel called to take up and the ideals of the religious life should take into consideration the age, the psycho-social and academic background of these candidates.

It is the practice of some institutes that after postulancy, the candidates are sent home to ponder what they have learned and experienced and to think over the implications. This is a very important practice that should be well exploited for the formation of the candidates. They should go home with some questions to reflect on especially those concerning the significant demands that the vocation will make on them. They should not just reflect about their vocation; they should also talk to their parents, brothers and sisters about their plans, the style of their life, and the demands of the charism of the congregation, and what it might mean for the family, especially the renunciations. When they come back for the remaining part of the formation period, it is necessary to find out the following from them:

- How they feel about their vocation and all it entails for their family and community?

- How the family members feel about it? What they say, specifically? How the parents and siblings reacted? Were they excited or discouraged? Why? It is absolutely important to know why the family members or relatives are discouraged or excited about their son or daughter becoming a religious. Some family members could get excited because they are going to have one of theirs become a priest, brother or sister. And the candidate is already given special treatment. Or it could be that the family members discourage the candidate because they feel the vocation is a waste of one's life.

- Why does the candidate insist on continuing in the vocation? Formators should be able to distinguish when a young man or woman is giving a trite and rehearsed talk, and when he or she is speaking what she earnestly desires out of conviction.

- What does the candidate gain and lose in choosing to continue in the religious life and in the particular religious family? What will be his or her greatest challenge? The more specific the responses to the questions the better. General and non-specific questions are not usually very helpful in matters like this.

- In all the responses given to these questions, formators should watch out how the candidates are able to justify their answers from their personal understanding and not simply from what they hear other people say.

Having followed the candidates thoroughly during this period, the formator is reasonably convinced of the good disposition of the candidates towards the vocation despite the conflicts or the ruptures that this will bring in their lives and for their families and communities. Attention should be paid to the tendency of the candidates to annul the tension between the ideals of the Christian vocation and needs and values that derive from their culture and personality.

Novitiate

The novitiate could be rightly called the definitive period for serious spiritual formation and acquisition of the identity of the religious family in terms of its charism and apostolate. The candidates are introduced into the lifestyle of the family through their written materials, such as their constitution, rules and customs, and the writings of their founders and followers. What they learn from these documents, they begin to practice systematically in the novitiate.

The candidates are accompanied personally to deepen their relationship with the Lord, increase their knowledge of themselves, their unique gifts and weaknesses, and are assisted to work on those aspects of their personality that will always tend to obstruct their willingness to give themselves fully to the Lord and to the religious family to which they belong. The conflicts experienced by each candidate some of which were noted during the postulancy, should be further explored and understood more during this time. When a conflict occupies a central place in the motivational system of a candidate, it means that such a candidate will have to spend undue energy to service that conflict. Issues relating to self-acceptance (including body image, intellectual giftedness, creative capacities, etc.), relational and emotional tendencies, self-perception, the content of self-ideal, and how these interplay in the candidate's relationship with God and with others, are absolutely important to know about each candidate during this period.

At the expiration of the first year of novitiate (most congregations have a two year novitiate program) novitiate directors or directresses should be able to know to a reasonable extent the kind of relationship that exists between each candidate and God as well as his or her affective attachment to the religious family. Is the candidate's relationship with God central in his or her life? Do they feel at home in this religious family or do they feel alienated or like visitors or merely as members of a group without any emotional connection? I have seen not a few religious men and women who have remained aloof and felt alienated from their religious family even after many years. Some others have no real emotional connection to the religious family. They see themselves as belonging to a kind of cooperation which they do not mind exploiting because it does not really concern them. This emotional condition is not helpful either to the individual or to the religious institute in question. This is why it is important to evaluate the kind of emotional attachment a candidate feels towards the religious family.

Towards the end of the novitiate, the questions posed to the candidates during the postulancy could be repeated to these candidates, to see how far they have grown in their own self-understanding and in the acquisition of their vocational identity.

Temporary Profession

If the periods of postulancy and novitiate were utilized so well for the formation of the candidates, the period of temporary profession would be less a period of terror and humiliation as it is in some institutes especially the female ones. From my own experience with some institutes, this period does not have any formational value for many people because the manner in which it is conceptualized by some religious institutes is so degrading and humiliating. The junior professed are often constantly reminded that they are nobody, and that their life is still hanging in the air, and that any slight mistake could take them out of the institute. Knowing the effect of all this, some of the temporarily professed live through the six to nine years in constant fear and terror. A good number of them do everything possible to wait for the time to be admitted finally into the family so that they can avenge for all the pains they went through as junior professed. Obviously, this frame of mind is closed to any kind of formation that is expected to take place during this period. This is not the mind of the Church for establishing this stage in the formation of the consecrated persons in the Church.

Yet, this stage is a very important one in the life of the religious. After the intense and secluded period of novitiate, the newly professed come out to test their newly acquired self and vocational identity in the real world, made of real people in the place of the apostolate and in the community. Those areas of strength and weakness, relational and emotional tendencies and the centrality of one's relationship with the Lord will all be put to test. It is during this period that those deriving from the culture and one's personality are experienced anew and in various forms. Being conversant with the specific issues about each junior professed (from the report of the Novice Master or Mistress), the formators in charge of them will be better placed to assist them in the new challenges and difficulties they meet during this period of their formation. It is expected that the junior professed should be able to share with their formators their experiences, challenges, difficulties and especially the areas they experience heightened tension in their lives. But the formators should make themselves trustable. For this reason, it is not wise to have just one person in charge of the junior professed when they are many.

The transition from the life in the novitiate to the life in the community is not always easy. This has to be recognized. Therefore both the junior professed and those in charge of them should try to understand the difficulties involved in this transition and so work through it. The goal of this stage of formation is not simply to wait for the time to be finally professed. On the contrary, it is the time of constant dialogue between the individual and the real experiences in the community and the place of the apostolate and the structures of the institute. All these experiences are placed in the context of the individual's experience of and relationship with God and with the religious family. While the religious family is examining the individual as to his or her suitability as a definitive member, the individual should also be examining himself or herself as to whether he or she is in the right place.

I am sure that if this stage of formation is utilized well by both the candidates and the institutes, it will be of great benefit to the individual and the religious family. Further issues concerning this stage shall be touched in the next section that deals with discernment of vocations in our communitarian African cultures. The period of ongoing formation has already been touched on in chapter two of this book. This is the period that the candidates should be accompanied in their own process of consolidating on the new identity they have acquired as religious and mourning the renunciations that this vocation entails, so that they will be more interiorly free to give themselves to the apostolate and be more suitable for final profession in the religious family. There are other aspects of the period of annual profession to consider – e.g. where full-time studies fit in; what sort of community and ministry experiences are desirable; what sort of evaluation processes are in place for vow renewal, and for asking for final profession, that will be conducive to ongoing formation, so that evaluation is not just an ordeal to be survived.

Chapter Six
Discernment of Vocations

Discerning Vocations: the Subjective and the Objective Levels

In general, discernment is an art by which we try to make good decisions when we are faced with choices. There would be no need for discernment if the course of action to take were always clear. Real life situations are often a tangle of issues, desires, emotions and aspirations. Discernment is important in the life of every Christian. At the heart of the Christian calling is the commitment to do the will of God. Christians who live a life of prayer realize the importance of discernment in their daily lives because they want to nurture the relationship they have with God; and so, they want to know and do God's will because they know that God always has their best interests at heart (Kiechle, 2005). This notwithstanding, knowing the will of God in particular circumstances is not easy. There are so many voices that it is not always easy to know the voice of God; there are many lights that it is not always easy to know the light of Christ. In the context of vocation to the priesthood or religious life, discernment is ascertaining whether the voice that one hears is God's voice or the voice of one's parents, oneself etc. In this context therefore, the notion of discernment necessarily implies the search for ways and means of determining the will of God (Wolff, 2003).

In discerning vocations to the priesthood and the consecrated life, all those involved – the candidates, the formators, the religious institute or the diocese – are just doing the same thing: they are seeking God's will for this individual regarding the priesthood and the particular religious family. They are asking whether this individual, this candidate, is actually suitable for this state of life – the priesthood or the consecrated life, and in a particular religious family or diocese. Discernment is an ongoing process whose beginning are often hidden in the mystery of God. For example, some feel called to the priesthood or religious life because a chance meeting with someone stirred up in them the desire or because someone suggested to them that they have the looks, the gait and mannerisms of priests etc. These events may move the candidate to apply to the seminary or the religious congregation so that the Church, through those entrusted with this task will discern with them whether they are being called. If accepted, this is seen as indicative that God has called them to embark on the journey of formation and ongoing discernment. However, there comes the decisive moment when the formators have to make decision as to whether a candidate should continue to the next stage of formation or not. That moment is important and all the dealings of the formators with the candidates will feed into this moment of decision-making.

We can distinguish two interconnected spheres at which discernment of vocation takes place: the first sphere is that of the personal. The individual engages in his/her own discernment. That is to say, each candidate should go through the process of discernment and discover whether this is his or her vocation. Basically, the individual has to make the decision of becoming a diocesan priest or a religious man or woman. This is the personal sphere of discerning vocations. But as the candidates ask themselves vital questions regarding their vocation, those entrusted with their training are also asking their own questions as to whether the candidates are suitable for the vocation; that is, whether they actually have the vocation. This is the institutional sphere where those who form the candidates make decisions about the suitability of those candidates according to the criteria or standards given by the Church for the formation of priests and candidates to the consecrated life.

Discernment of vocations in the institutional sphere already starts when the candidates are selected and admitted into formation. That is why there should be continuity from one stage of formation to the next, so that consistent information concerning a candidate's tendencies, values and attitudes can be gathered and contribute to discernment that are more objective. This kind of information helps to reduce a lot of uncertainty and ambiguity about a candidate, and so makes decision about him or her less subjective.

With the ongoing discernment taking place, there comes a moment when formators have to make the concrete decision whether a candidate should continue in formation or not. It is a very important and delicate task. It is not something to play with. Some formators often see the period of decision-making (or screening as some call it) as a time to demonstrate the authority they have over the candidates. For some others, it is a moment to defend the candidates of their choice. These attitudes actually defeat the aim and process of discernment. They betray ignorance of the delicacy of this matter. Discernment is so important because it is the good of the individual and that of the Church that is at stake in this process. Careless approaches to this process could lead to admission to profession and ordination of self-serving individuals for whom God is secondary in their lives, and rejection of persons with genuine dispositions to give their lives totally to God and to the Church. More than anything, the formators who discern the vocation of the candidates need to possess certain requisite knowledge and internal dispositions corresponding to the delicate nature of this exercise.

Requisites for Proper Discernment of Vocations

A primary requisite for the proper discernment of vocations is an attitude of awareness of and prayerful respect for the delicacy of this exercise. Formators carry out the discernment in the name of God and of the Church and they are making decisions that would definitely impact on the lives of other people - the candidates and those they will encounter in life. Therefore it is absolutely important that they have the true desire to seek God's will and the good of the Church in that process. That is why this moment of exercise should be preceded by a period of prayerful solitude and reflection by each formator. They pray personally but also as a group, asking God for light and grace to be open to the promptings of the Holy Spirit in their deliberations and subsequent decision. It is absolutely important they are not overtaken by personal interests (Wolff, 2003). When some formators boast before the candidates that they will punish them during the time of deciding on their promotion or expulsion, they are actually saying that they are not interested in seeking God's will as regards these candidates. In other words, they are saying that they are not interested in discerning the vocation of the candidates but in muscling their way through to make good their threat. In some major seminaries, this is a common occurrence. It also happens that some novice directors and some of those in charge of the junior professed remind them that they (the directors) have their (the candidates') destiny in their hands. Such arrogant display of power and intimidation indicate indisposition to seek the will of God for the concerned candidate(s). In such instances, it is the *ego* of the formators that stands out and takes the place of God and the Church. Such attitude should be seen by formators as completely out of place in the process of discerning vocations.

In addition to this, it is also absolutely necessary that the formators are agreed on what they are doing when they are discerning or deciding on the vocation of the candidates. As part of this, it is important that the group discerning should have formulated written aims and criteria in order to be as objective and clear as they can about what they are doing and what the criteria are. Wolff (2003) emphatically observes that discernment is not possible for a group of formators if they do not share the same aim at the deepest level. If formators come to the discernment exercise with the disposition to defend some candidates or punish others, this fundamental aim is defeated although, we believe that God, in his infinite wisdom, still can permit and work with such human sinfulness to achieve the divine purpose. This issue will be further elaborated on later in this chapter.

Having said this, I will now look at some other requirements which are in discerning vocations.

The Objective or Substantive Criteria

This requirement has two sides, the spiritual and the human. The spiritual part constitutes the core of the vocational identity of the priest or consecrated person. It also includes the canonical requirements for being a priest or a consecrated person. Therefore, the formators should actually know what the Church is looking for in suitable candidates for the priesthood, and what a particular religious order is looking for in its prospective members. This entails a profound knowledge of the theology of the priesthood and of the consecrated life as well as the lifestyle of the particular religious order. It is the life and teachings of Jesus Christ that form the foundation of the life of the priest and the consecrated person. So, the formators should be able to know the primary motivations of the candidates, and whether these motivations are constituted of the values of the Christian vocation such as love of God, service of others, self-gift expressed in the counsels, genuine sense of commitment to God, personal relationship with the Lord, love of the Church in her mission and sacramental life, etc. Notice that these motives are primarily *other*-centered; they relate to self-transcendence in love of God. There should be clear evidence in the lives of the candidates that these values constitute their primary motives for the priesthood or the consecrated life.

Since human motivations are always mixed, the candidates could have other motives such as further education, social prestige, safety, financial security, improving the social and financial status of one's family and fear of family responsibility, but these should remain secondary and exert less energy in the motivational system of the candidates. Moreover, the formation process should aid such candidates to acquire the desire for ongoing purification of motives so that these secondary self-serving motives are gradually extirpated.

When these self-serving motives are the primary motives in a candidate, it means the candidate is using the vocation for his or her self-enhancement. Self-serving motives obstruct self-donation which the Christian vocation demands. The preponderance in the Christian vocation of persons for whom this set of values constitutes their primary motives is the major source of the many problems in the priesthood and the consecrated life[2]. Inability to satisfy these self-serving motives in the vocation can lead to a lot of frustration and meaninglessness in the priests and religious men and women while satisfaction of these motives is usually at a high cost to the people of God and to the ideals of the priesthood and religious life. That is why it is important to make sure that the primary motives are the values of the Christian vocation. As the candidates strengthen and nurture these primary motives, the secondary ones will overtime lose their power, and be integrated into the primary motives (Kiechle, 2005). When this is happening, it indicates that the priest or religious is growing in his or her vocation. This

---

[2] In his speech to the priests of Awka Diocese, Nigeria, on September 6, 2010, the then Apostolic Administrator, now the Bishop of Awka Diocese, Most Rev. Paulinus Ezeokafor expressed his displeasure over the priests' refusal to pool funds together in order to assist the priests in disadvantaged parishes. The major reason the priests gave for their refusal is that it would make priests not work hard any more since they would simply hope on their salary. In other words, pooling funds together will mean removing the incentive for which some of them do the priestly work. The bishop expressed his displeasure in these words: "My dear Msgr and Frs., if these fears are real, then our presbyterium is in deep trouble. It means that the majority of us engage in ministry just because of the pecuniary benefits so much that if funds were to be centralized they would lose the incentive to work. Does it mean my dear Msgr. & Frs., that people will so easily lose the sense of the priesthood as a vocation because funds are pooled together and then distributed to all? Does it mean that many of us have not imbibed what St. Peter said to the presbyters about giving a shepherd's care to the flock of God, *'not simply as a duty but gladly, as God wants; not for sordid money but because you are eager to do it'?*(1 Pt. 5:2). Indeed, the excerpts from the reports are sad commentaries on the attitude of all of us as priests". See his speech titled, "See I lay in Zion a Stone, A Precious Cornerstone for a Sure Foundation (Is. 28:16", 5. This is just an example of what happens when many in the Christian vocation have self-serving motives as their primary motives. They generally turn the vocations into businesses or opportunities to be exploited to the full. The spiritual foundation of the vocation is lost in the process.

constant integration of motives, which leads to experience of focused life and wholeness, is the major goal of ongoing formation. But formators will have to determine the possibility of such an integration of motives taking place through the attitudes and the life the candidate is living.

Every formator therefore should ask himself or herself questions as these: Does this candidate have a conscious relationship with the Lord? How do I know? What is the nature of this relationship? How important is this relationship in his or her life? What are evidences that indicate that there is or there is not such a conscious relationship? These kinds of questions are helpful to the formators in assessing their own knowledge of the candidates and the values that constitute the core of Christian vocational identity. This touches again on the question of criteria I mentioned above. It also raises the problem of how to "verify" the criteria. Behavioural evidence is part of the criteria but, more importantly, there is need to know the *persona* that deploys those acts; what moves this person, what is at the center of his or her life and the extent to which the love of God and of the Church are constitutive of these. This is an issue that the formators should have discussed and worked on among themselves.

On the human aspect, the formators should know the human qualities the Church is looking for in the candidates, such as have been given in the documents of the Church (See Chapter One). Here, the formators should be able to know the personalities of the candidates, their affective responsiveness, relational abilities, and how these generally impact their lives and that of others. Again, they should be able to examine the situation of each candidate well with evidence. A helpful question a formator could ask himself or herself is this: Considering the history and personality of this candidate, is it likely or unlikely that he or she will be able to live this life meaningfully without too many problems? I know a lady who wanted to enter religious life. She has a highly entrenched paranoid style of perceiving and relating with people. Her history shows she does not have any friends because she cannot trust anyone. But she prays, loves the Lord and wants to give herself in service of the poor. My advice to her was that it would be much easier for her to join any of the secular institutes, if she so wished, where she could live on her own and still be a consecrated person. She rejected my advice and applied to an institute that accepted her. One week to her admission into the novitiate, she left the institute because the sisters were not good and trustworthy enough. Considering her personality and history, community life would be very difficult for her and for those she is going to live with. This kind of information is very important in making decision about the suitability of a candidate.

The Inner Freedom of the Formators

Formators should do their best to grow in freedom which allows them the emotional distance they need to carry out this sensitive task of discernment. This requirement would not have been necessary if human beings were perfect, and completely open to truth. But because we are imperfect beings entrusted with such a delicate matter, we must do our best to be aware of our inner blocks and prejudices which usually interfere with discernment and right judgment. The more we are aware of our prejudices or biases and how they manifest themselves, then we can control them, and so, allow the Holy Spirit to guide us in the discernment process. Obviously, to gain this awareness implies that the formators live genuine lives of prayer and are present to themselves, their emotions and beliefs towards the candidates. If prejudices or biases are not recognized and controlled, they can lead to much emotional violence on the candidates and on the discernment process. Prejudices are common among us human beings and formators should be honest enough to recognize and acknowledge them, as well as see how they influence their relationship with persons especially the candidates, so as to minimize the harm, hurt or trauma caused because of them. We can note three particular forms of prejudice or bias.

Bias from Personality

This kind of bias comes from the idiosyncrasies that derive from our self-concept and inclinations. A formator, for instance, who is overcome by feelings of inadequacy could be easily intimidated by intelligent, assertive, and independent minded candidates. Such formators will tend to see these candidates as stubborn and arrogant, lacking in humility, and therefore, not capable of living a life of obedience. Formators with very low self-esteem can use their position as formators to feed their need for self-importance. They prefer the candidates who do not ask biting questions, and who are sheepishly subservient. Questions are often construed by such formators as aimed at humiliating them and therefore offensive and punishable. This is even worse if the formator is not aware of it or is unable to control its manifestation. An example can illustrate this point very clearly. A novice directress in a female congregation constantly compared herself with her novices. She would be very antagonistic towards the candidates she felt were more beautiful than herself. Very beautiful women were her target, and few of them would survive to make their first religious profession. Whenever she expelled any of them, she would give the reason that their beauty made them arrogant and that they had wayward tendencies! The offence of these candidates was just their physical beauty, which the formator was obsessed with.

Some formators have an extreme need for admiration and praise. Candidates who praise them are easily promoted to the next stage of formation, while others who do not, could be expelled sometimes with the description, "they are not sensitive to their environment". Such formators are easily fooled and manipulated by clever candidates who are always ready to flatter these formators. Obviously, the need for admiration and praise does not permit the formator to distinguish truth about himself or herself from flattery. What is important is admiration and praise. Some formators crave the love of the candidates to such an extent that they lack the necessary emotional distance to make reasonable decision about the candidates

In these instances the wall built by *ego needs* and biases from personality tend to obstruct the discernment process. If the formator does not know this or does not even care, it is very likely that some persons who can be adjudged to be suitable candidates for the priesthood or consecrated life are expelled and less suitable ones admitted. Unconsciously, the criteria of discernment have been changed and the primary criterion will be who and what makes the formator(s) comfortable and happy.

Group Bias

This is a set of biases that has its root in the group on grounds such as ethnic identity, race, language, diocese, country, region or town of origin, etc. Such can exert serious negative influence on the discernment process. Here a blind eye is turned to the criteria of love of God and the values of Christian vocation and the focus of attention is the group the candidate belongs to. Some formators are protective of the candidates from their own ethnic or language group, race, diocese, region of origin etc. but are terribly critical of those from other ethnic groups or races. In other instances, the fight is against candidates from certain dioceses. Formators who develop soft spots for candidates from a particular group tend to overlook unhealthy and sometimes dangerous attitudes and values of those candidates. The same is the case with formators who tend to stereotype candidates from particular group – race, language, ethnicity, diocese or region.

This bias can be very strong in formation. It manifests itself in form of ethnicism, diocesanism, townism (people coming from the same town), racism, etc. The power of group bias in formation is the basic reason why candidates as well as priests and religious men and women are worried about the group the formators belong. Often, Christian vocationers do not ask whether a formator is suitable for formation; the first question is about where the formator comes from, and whether he or she comes from *our* group. This preoccupation with groups and the attendant biases are very real. Sadly, they are destroying many presumably genuine vocations and promoting many self-serving individuals to the priesthood and the religious life. In international congregations, it is race and ethnic origin that are often the major source of problem. In some, however, an unhealthy alliance is built between some groups against others. This unhealthy condition in formation houses can be extended to life in communities and dioceses. Overtime, priests and religious men and women spend more time talking about problems deriving from group bias than about their own conversion and growth. This is a common experience in many formation houses, dioceses and communities.

It is therefore important for the formators to recognize their individual and common group biases. It is dangerous to politicize the discernment process. That is why it is absolutely necessary for formators not to consult with one another before the time of discernment or try to persuade others ahead of time. On this point, someone involved in formation drew my attention to the need sometimes to lobby other formators in order to mobilize bias against other formators in the service of what is perceived to be good and true. This goes to underline what have been said above about the need for formators to be open and self-conscious of their prejudices and biases. The presence of formators who are blind to their biases creates a difficult situation for other formators and candidates.

Ideological Bias

This bias derives from two needs found in all human beings, namely security and adventure. We have the need to feel secured and safe. At the same time, we have the need to move out of our security and deal with new challenges and experiences in our lives. These two fundamental needs are equally important for our survival as individuals and as humankind. Tradition and orthodoxy provide us with the security and safety we need to understand the many complexities of human life. At the same time, events and circumstances force us out of the conserved security into new frontiers that could be anything but certain. As we grow from childhood, we generally tend towards one of the two extremes, depending usually, on the way we were raised and the ideological preferences of our significant others.

Dealing with these two needs in human life and social adaptation has over the centuries led to the development of two ideological bents that appear to be in opposition to each other.

Thus, we have the conservative ideology that focuses attention on the maintenance of tradition and the rules that preserve it. This ideology emphasizes stability and order and views of some elements in history as normative and sacrosanct. The progressive ideology tends to court novelty and at one extreme of its spectrum are the revisionists who commit themselves to the revisability of any and every tenet of life because every 'truth' is held to be provisional. Progressives emphasize freedom and change. Surely, this is an oversimplification of a complex issue. But, it does give us some insight into the differences among human beings as regards their inclination to emphasize permanence or change and how our ideological bias affects how we think, feel, and relate with others. Our maturity as individuals invites us to integrate these two needs of our lives. The more rigidly entrenched we are in any of these two ideological tendencies, the more harmful we can be to ourselves and to others, as well as to society.

Formators need to be aware of their ideological tendency and how it influences their attitude towards and decisions on the candidates. Some formators are inclined towards defending the status quo without expending energy and time to consider the rationale of any novelty introduced. Such may fight significant changes in the formation house and they may tend to suspect candidates who seem to be very spontaneous and adaptable to circumstances. These formators insist that things should be done the way they have always been done. The emphasis is not on the truthfulness and validity of the issue concerned, but rather on the fact that it has always been so. This is basically one of the reasons why the cultural aspect of formation is largely neglected in certain formation houses. It is also the reason why some houses of formation still keep the formation programs that are outdated and that have little relevance to the cultural and present circumstances, despite what the documents of the Church say in this regard.

These formators suspect candidates who appear to be open to questions that challenge the status quo. Instead of accompanying and supporting these candidates in the task of integrating the new element into the old and the traditional, they attack these candidates and accuse them of having no respect for the way the Christian vocation is conceptualized and lived.

Some formators who are coloured with the progressive stripe can be so broad-minded that everything is up for renegotiation including the standards against which attitudes and values of the candidates are to be assessed. The emphasis is on new energy, new ideas and new visions won in dialogue with the ever changing context of the modern world. The Christian vocation is often interpreted solely in terms of service to the poor, rather than establishing the pre-eminence of the God as the leit-motif from which the service of the poor derives its meaning and direction. Without the dominance of this God-perspective, the apostolate can be turned into avenues of self-promotion and self-adoration. These two ideological tendencies could be traced to two divergent views about the human situation. The "conservative" tendency focuses on the fallibility of human nature, while the "liberal" tendency sees the innate goodness of people and the possibility of human perfectibility.

To check this kind of bias, it is absolutely important for the formators to be aware of the need to honour both change and permanence. The foundational teachings of the Church regarding the priesthood and the consecrated life as mediated by the charism of the congregation and policies of the dioceses etc. remain normative in the discernment process but there should be openness to emergent and contextual realities that may throw new light on the normative elements and legitimize new ways of acting. This mental framework would prepare the formators to carefully weigh every element including the new without throwing them out simply because they are new or traditional as the case may be. This attitude amounts to recognition that the Holy Spirit blows wherever it wills without ceasing to remain the Spirit of Christ. It is therefore important that formators encourage candidates to inhabit the space created by the generative tension between permanence and change in order to value what is permanent while being open to change and newness. This attitude is based on the fact that the values of the Christian vocation transcend ideological leanings. It is the self-giving love embodied in the life of Jesus Christ, a love that leads each of us to self-transcendence to that beauty so ancient and yet so new, as St. Augustine describes God in *The Confessions*.

The Use, Timing and Abuse of Psychological Evaluation in Discernment

If "the human dimension is the foundation of all formation" (PDV, n. 7), then it is important that candidates for the priesthood and the consecrated life be persons with reasonably mature personality. This basically refers to the absence of mental disorder and presence of reasonable affective maturity (CCE, 2008, n. 2). Psychological evaluation or assessment is an important tool in detecting certain psychological defects which could be a source of many problems for the future priest or consecrated person and the Church. First, it is an important tool in detecting psychological defects that are pathological, and which may reveal itself in due time. Persons with psychopathology could be screened out early enough so that they could seek professional help and the insights gained from the assessment put to use in helping others.

It is important to note that psychological evaluation does not aim simply at identifying cases of psychopathology among the candidates. It is also helpful in describing the psychological structure of the candidates and how the various components of the psyche interact in their overall psychological functioning. This description is absolutely important for it furnishes information concerning the underlying motivations, strengths and weaknesses of the candidates and the psychological strategies they employ in coping psychologically. It has to give information about the candidates' self-concept and self-estimation, and how the self is usually maintained in human interactions. This kind of information will provide indications on the basis of which it could be said that the candidate could grow in self-giving to the Lord according to the state of life demanded by the priesthood and the consecrated life. The emphasis here is on the candidate's *capacity to internalize* the values of the vocation, and be a channel of the Good News to the people of God and not its obstruction! This means that only psychologists who share the vision of human person by Christian anthropology should be allowed to carry out such evaluations of the candidates for the priesthood and the religious life (CCE, 2008, n. 6).

The information gathered from psychological assessment is used by formators in understanding and accompanying the candidates during the period of formation. From the psychological assessment, formators should be able to draw up the formational path of each candidate according to each person's needs and follow them as such. Where necessary, experts could be invited to accompany the candidates during their formation so as to facilitate the healing of psychic wounds (CCE, 2008, n. 9). For instance, persons who have a rigid sense of responsibility that tends to dry up spontaneity could be helped to loosen up and develop some degree of emotional attachment in relationships, including and not least in relationship to the Lord. Those who tend to be too emotional and superficial in their understanding of life could be assisted to acquire some degree of discipline that is needed to think more deeply. The acquisition of these developmental skills goes hand in hand with growth in self-knowledge. From one stage of formation to another, formators will be able to keep track of how the candidates are growing.

This implies that if psychological assessment is to be used well, it needs to be carried out at an appropriate time in the formation of the candidates. In fact, the CCE states: "Right from the moment when the candidate presents himself for admission to the seminary, the formator needs to be able accurately to comprehend his personality; potentialities, dispositions, and the types of psychological wounds, evaluating their nature and intensity" (n. 7). This kind of knowledge is facilitated by proper psychological evaluation of the candidates by competent experts. This means that there is an appropriate time to carry out the psychological evaluation of the candidates to assist formators right away in understanding the candidates better.

Following this guideline therefore, I believe that the best time to carry out psychological evaluation for those training for the diocesan priesthood is either the moment the candidates are admitted into the spiritual year or before being admitted to the spiritual year. What is important here is that the spiritual year be fully utilized in verifying the capacity of the candidates to grow in the vocation and accompanying them on the journey of self-awareness and human integration.

It is also suggested that a second psychological assessment be done for the candidates before they enter into the stage of theological formation. The aim of this second assessment is to see how far the candidates have grown in the achievement of their vocational identity, and how reasonably aware and open they are to themselves and to their own human and vocational development. It is also very important to observe the kind of impact philosophical studies has made in their sense of self in relation to the vocation they feel called to. Attention should be paid to how far the candidates have succeeded in consolidating their self-identity, and how the values of priestly vocation relate to this self-identity. This second evaluation should be able to indicate how the individual is managing his difficulties in relation to the values of the vocation. This second evaluation should be compared with the first one, and differences be indicated. If after all the help given by the formators and experts and the efforts of a candidate, this second evaluation indicates that the candidate is still "unable to face realistically his areas of grave immaturity", such as "strong affective dependencies, notable lack of freedom in relations, excessive rigidity of character, lack of loyalty, uncertain sexual identity, deep-seated homosexual tendencies, etc.', it is very likely that the "path of formation for such a candidate "will have to be terminated" (CCE, n.10).

For those being formed for the consecrated life, postulancy seems to me to be the best time to do the assessment. Some institutes carry out the evaluation before admitting the candidates into novitiate. Again, any of the two options is still good. The novitiate is the time of intense formation during which the information gathered from psychological assessment could be amply utilized in accompanying the candidates. What is said in the preceding paragraphs apply here. However, towards the end of the novitiate stage of formation, a test such as *Stories of Imagined*

Future, which is a projective test developed to ascertain the maturity of Christian vocationers, could be administered to the candidates to see how they have progressed in their vocational journey. It is assumed that this test was among the battery of tests used during the first assessment, so that the second result could be compared with the first. In this context, the value of the period of temporary vows becomes obvious, for it is the time of consolidation of already acquired vocational identity according to the particular religious family.

From all that has been said in this section, it does not seem appropriate to carry out psychological evaluation of the candidates just few months before the final profession or diaconate ordination, unless in a situation of obvious unhealthy manifestation of psychological deficiencies that call for deeper understanding. After all, a candidate nearing diaconate in most parts of Africa has spent at least between seven and eight years in formation after secondary school. The religious persons, especially women, have stayed a minimum of six years after their first profession. This unfortunate timing of evaluation sends out the message that the major concern of the Superiors is just to look out for those to dismiss and it turns the evaluation into a type of "final exam" that has to be passed, thus raising anxiety levels and lowering the openness to truthful sharing about self. Sometimes, the Superiors manipulate the psychological reports and use them as reasons to dismiss those they had already decided in advance to get rid of. They are just looking for someone – an expert – to carry the blame. Sometimes the reports of the experts are distorted to fit their original decision. This is a serious matter of abuse of psychological evaluation, and it is also a violation of the candidates. The CCE clearly cautions that formators (and superiors) should *suggest* psychological evaluation for the candidates in such a way as to avoid "the impression that such a suggestion is the prelude to the candidate's inevitable dismissal from the seminary or house of formation" (n. 12). This leads me to the important issue regarding the dismissal of candidates in a communitarian culture.

The Fear and Shame of Being Dismissed in a Communitarian Culture

There is a great need for formators and Superiors to be more sensitive to the communitarian dimension of the African people in the formation and discernment of vocations to the priesthood and the religious life. Often, this lack of sensitivity results in reckless treatment of Christian vocationers, and leaves behind much anger and rancour, and, in some instances, even despair. This call for greater sensitivity is a demand of Christian justice and charity. All that it requires is thorough and timely termination of the discernment process where need be, so that people are not exposed to so much shame and fear, which will make it so hard for them to get reintegrated back into their various communities.

African cultures are primarily communitarian. Psychologically, this means that self-esteem is a function not merely of individual abilities but especially of societal acceptance and belonging. This situation can be a source of enormous psychological stress to the candidates for the priesthood and the religious life. But it does not have to be so if we do well what we should do as formators of these men and women. As things stand today, many Africans, even the literate ones, do not understand that a seminarian in minor seminary, for instance, is a young man growing up and still faces decisional challenges as to what he feels he is called to be. In the same way, most people do not understand the difference between temporary and final vows. All they know is that their son or daughter has been professed, and that is it! They do not understand that a temporarily professed sister is still under discernment as to whether she will definitively be admitted to the religious family. What they do know is that "this young woman is in the convent". In the marriage symbolism, it means that "she has been married out", just as an ordained priest or a professed brother has also been "married"! In all these cases, their marriage is to God.

This socio-psychological situation already pressurizes some of the candidates to do everything within their power to stay whether they feel called or not. Reaching ordination or profession for some candidates becomes a much more stressful preoccupation than facing the challenges of personal growth that formation offers. This could be one of the reasons behind the attitude of some Igbo seminarians described by late Archbishop A.K. Obiefuna: "Every candidate considers himself called. He acts and even claims to have received the call directly from God. How often do we not hear from the candidates, 'I am sure I am meant to be a priest' and this even when all the human and spiritual gifts necessary for any authentic vocation to the priesthood are clearly absent" (1993). Behind this apparent desperation could be fear of social rejection and shame were one to leave or be dismissed.

A life lived like this often leads to some form of motivational alienation, in which a candidate may feel so pressured that he or she is unable to take a position or give a personal evaluation of a situation. This situation also gives too much psychological power to some formators to instil fears in the candidates and intimidate them. Knowing that their dismissal will be a social disaster for the candidates, a psychologically immature formator may cash in on it, consciously or unconsciously, and be a perpetual threat to the candidates (Ike, 1993). Thus, the formative environment could be charged with such emotional apprehensiveness which does not allow the formators the psychological and spiritual freedom they need to send away a student who is considered not fit for the vocation. It sometimes creates room for compromises and sympathies that are destructive of the formation process and the seminarians themselves. This can be seen in some attitudes of the formators who swear to leave the seminary if a particular seminarian is sent away or not, depending on the situation.

The reader can now appreciate why most ex-seminarians and ex-religious men and women are often scorned by their people. They carry some kind of shame around them, as if they committed a crime. Sometimes, parents and relatives make fun of them. And if they are not doing well in their career, people tend to attribute their condition to a curse placed on them for leaving or being sent away from the seminary or convent. Yet it could be the challenge of adjusting back to another state of life after spending many years in the seminary or in the religious life that is the stumbling block in their lives. I know of some ladies who having been dismissed from the religious life wear dresses designed in imitation of religious habits although they belong to no congregation.

At the profession or ordination of these women and men, the community to which they belong is fully present. All the relatives, near and far, the villagers and townspeople, join hands together in jubilation and celebration. The family of the ordained and the professed receive special attention that day. It is a festive occasion, as festive as any traditional marriage ceremonies in Africa. The person who is making the religious profession or being ordained is part and parcel of the community.

Now, this cultural situation should make formators, dioceses and Institutes of Consecrated Life appreciate the social import of dismissing a candidate from the seminary or the house of formation at certain stages in their formation. The more the number of years already spent on the journey to the priesthood or religious life, the more difficult it is to leave because, among other things, the heavier the shame and disappointment. What I am going to suggest in the next section concerns how to deal with social shame that can and should be avoided, especially through careful discernment right from the time a candidate makes application to be admitted to a congregation or to a diocese.

Practical Guidelines for Dismissing Candidates in Communitarian Culture

An important point to realize is that marriage is very important for Africans and constitutes part of their self-definition as male or female. Africans marry, in the main, to beget children. Age of marriage for the Africans means the age at which someone will be able to have children. So, it is simply not fair to waste a woman's time in the convent only to dismiss her after so many years without very serious reasons. This means that formators and superiors of Institutes of Consecrated life should have it at the back of their mind to do everything possible to be able to come to moral certitude about the suitability of any candidate, especially women, so that "her time" is not wasted unnecessarily. In this regard:

- It is crucial that serious and fundamental discernment be done at the period of *postulancy*, so that when one is admitted into the novitiate, there is the greater possibility that she is known well enough to be given appropriate accompaniment that she needs. If appropriate discernment is done during this time of formation, it should make further discernment in the novitiate less cumbersome so that formators can admit candidates to first profession with some degree of assurance that they are making the right decision.

- Only those candidates about whom there is reasonable basis for belief in their openness to transformation could be sent to the novitiate for subsequent formation and further discernment. You do not send someone to the novitiate out of sympathy or just to continue to "try luck"! I am very much convinced that if proper attention is paid to the candidates during the novitiate, formators will have more solid ground to carry out their assessment of the candidates. It should be clear to the formator, in conscience and within the possibilities of being human, that the candidates proposed for religious profession should go on. It is unfair to allow a candidate to make the first religious profession when the formator has any reasonable doubt about their suitability for final vows. Sometimes, some formators confess, "I knew she would not make it"! If you knew she would not make it, you should not have allowed her to waste her time. This carelessness leaves a lot of bitterness in the lives of those women who leave the convent at a time they feel unable to get married or be integrated fully into the society.

- The period between temporary and final vows is often a nightmare, a time of incessant anxiety. It should not be. Institutes should try to see that only in grave cases should candidates not be admitted to final profession by being as thorough as possible as regards the discernment for admission into temporary vows. I think the key to reducing shame and fear (they can never be completely eliminated given cultural attitudes) is ensuring that young religious are given clear feedback so that they have time to address issues, knowing that the persistence of the same problems will mean they will NOT be allowed to keep renewing vows. In other words, in most cases, it should not be a big shock to someone to be told they are not being accepted to renew vows (or to make final vows). And they should also have serious reasons for this. It is just cruel to deny someone final profession as a demonstration of power. It is an example of abuse of power.

▪ Finally, when a candidate is sent away, it is important to let them know why they are sent away (as I said above, the person should be told long before they are sent away what the issues are, and they should be told that it could result in them being sent away). It is a mark of respect for the person, and it is also a protection of the person's self-image before others. Being fundamentally *a communitarian culture*, the individual does not live for herself, but as an essential member of the community. Effort should be made to communicate the information to the candidate in a kind and compassionate manner. In some cases, it is even necessary to involve the parents or significant others in the life of the person concerned. This strategy helps to lessen the impact of the social shame. It is not enough simply to give the person a letter or make it as a kind of announcement at a gathering. It does not seem right to care for the poor outside the convent while remaining unconcerned about the sister who is considered unfit to continue in the vocation.

These guidelines also apply to the discernment and dismissal of unsuitable candidates for the priesthood. The long years of priestly formation give formators the ample time they need for proper discernment of the vocations. The serious setback we have in Africa is that there is practically no continuity in the formation of diocesan priests except moving from one stage to another. As I suggested in chapter five of this book, if there is continuity in the knowledge of candidates from one stage of formation to the next, formators will have more accumulated knowledge on the basis of which to judge the suitability or unsuitability of candidates. Whenever there is serious doubt, decision should be made in favour of the Church (Canon 144).

At the end of the Spiritual Year, formators should be confident enough that the seminarians they are sending to the *Philosophicum* are open to formation and desirous of living the priestly life. Effort should be made at this stage to dismiss those with wrong and entrenched values that contradict the priestly lifestyle, especially if those are the primary motives of those candidates for entering the seminary. Those who are in the seminary because of their parents should also be helped to make their own decision. Those with entrenched psychological difficulties that need professional attention, should be attended to according to their needs, and should be certified to continue or discontinue after such professional help (CCE, 2008, n. 10). It is unfair to the individual and to the Church to promote to ordination or profession someone with obvious psychological difficulties that affect seriously the person's ability to live a meaningful life in the Christian vocation.

Philosophicum is undergraduate studies, and marks an important step in the journey to the priesthood. The points of growth in the life of each candidate should be properly assessed each year. By the time a seminarian finishes his philosophical studies, formators would be able to say that they could proceed to theological studies, with evidence of growth in the acquisition of their vocational identity. Academic abilities should not be the overriding criterion of assessment. This is the period to do a definitive assessment and dismiss with respect and explanation, those who are deemed not suitable for this life. It should be remembered that the suitability of candidates should be proved with positive and concrete points and all reasonable doubts should be excluded (Canon 1052).

Seminarians in theological studies have entered into the final stage of their formation to the priesthood. If honest and proper assessment was done in the previous stages, it is very unlikely that theology seminarians could be dismissed unless for a very serious reason. It is unfair to wait for a young man to reach the stage of theological studies before he is told that he is not fit for the priesthood because of one flaw in his character which was noticed as far back as when he was in the spiritual year. However, it is to be noted, too, that some problems only emerge in time, and the proximity to ordination may draw out of some seminarians certain attitudes and behaviours that were previously hidden and disguised. When this is the case, it should be obvious to the formators that this is indeed the situation. The important point in all this is that formators should not wait until near diaconate ordination before they become serious with their discernment. And when a candidate is dismissed, the candidate should be told why he is being dismissed. This should be done in such a way that formators are not trying to convince the person of something they do not want to hear. This can lead to fruitless arguments and resentment. Again, this is a mark of respect for the candidate, who is a child of God and son of the Church.

Final Remarks

The passion to write this book came from my love for the Church, her priests and consecrated persons who give themselves in a special way to the mission Jesus Christ entrusted to the Church. This book also comes from a deep cry in my heart about the deplorable condition of African people. I firmly believe that Catholic priests and consecrated persons, born in this great continent of Africa, can do much more to improve the condition of African people. But this can only happen if we are deeply true to the Lord and to the vocation He has called us to in the Church. God loves Africans, and a lot of missionary work has happened on the continent. Yet, poverty, endemic illnesses, bad leadership, and illiteracy have continued to plague this continent so that it continues to be in this 21st century a symbol of all that is not going well in the world. And almost all these problems are man-made: they stem from the plague of entrenched individual and group egoisms that underlie the corruption that has ravaged various nations of this continent. As Africans, we love life, family and children. But the massive corruption on the continent questions the sincerity of our love for life and for children. Only a love that gives itself in selflessness, such as has been shown in the person of Jesus Christ who is the model for our love as priests and religious, can lift this continent so that we can genuinely and in the Spirit of Jesus Christ care for its children. Blessed Mother Teresa of Calcutta would often say: "God loves you, God wants you, God needs you". This is the basic truth that needs to be experienced concretely by the African people.

African priests and consecrated persons should be at the forefront of this work of incarnating the love and care of God among the people of Africa. But as things stand, some priests and consecrated persons in Africa seem to have been more faithful to and concerned about themselves rather than to Jesus Christ, His ministry, the Church, and the enduring values of our African cultures. If some members of the clergy and the consecrated life had not been too close to the corrupt systems of our nations, I suppose there would have been more effective impact in the lives of our people and in their destiny. This is far from the mind of Christ and of the Church. This book is therefore a plea for a seasoned and conscientious attention to the formation of African priests and consecrated persons who will be ready to follow the Lord with their whole heart, mind and strength, despite their weaknesses. Good tree usually bears good fruit (Mt. 7:17). The desire is not for perfect priests and religious men and women. None exists in the whole world. What good formation does is that it will reinstate the preeminence of self-transcending values of the Gospel and diminish the impact of the self-serving values we have. As Father Terence Grant clearly states in his book, *The Silence of Unknowing*, "spiritual growth comes through self-transcendence, not from self-improvement. Christianity is not just another means to further our self-interest. If it were, we might as well close and lock the Church doors forever, because the world offers quicker and more gratifying ways to satisfy the demands of the self than we do. Christianity is, rather, a call to forget about the self, to move beyond self-interest as the motivation for what we do" (1995, pp. 50-51). This is the essence of Christian spiritual growth, because that is the life of Jesus Christ who, though he was divine, did not count equality with God something to be grasped, but emptied himself, taking the form of a servant, humbled himself by being obedient even unto death on the cross (Phil. 2. 6-8). Priests and consecrated men and women, through their commitment live a life of self-transcendence, which is anchored firmly in the relationship with Our Lord Jesus Christ. Our hope is that good formation will help the future priests and consecrated persons be more committed to self-transcendence in love in imitation of Christ and in solicitude for their brothers and sisters. It is only in this way that they can gradually positively influence the socio-cultural, economic and political structures, which have kept the continent on her knees and make it seem as if Africa cannot stand on her feet and take care of her own.

But it is not only about the African continent; it is also about the mission of the Church in the whole world. Africa is second to Asia in the number of vocations to the priesthood and the consecrated life. Europe and North America are increasingly becoming the Old World when it comes to Christian practice and vocations to the priesthood and the religious life. In his *Crossing the Threshold of Hope*, St. Pope John Paul II had said that "perhaps, one day, the words of Cardinal Hyacinth Thiandoum, who foresaw the possibility that the Old World would be evangelized by black missionaries, will prove true" (1994, p. 12). This is already happening with the many priests and religious men and women who are ministering in various countries in Europe and North America, as well as consecrated men and women of African origin who are involved in many apostolates and who also have injected new life into some religious orders that are near extinction. St. Pope John Paul II saw this new wave of missionary activity from the African continent as "evidence of the Church's renewed vitality" (p. 12). This is even the more reason why we need to give solid formation to the African priests and consecrated men and women. Then, they can be true witnesses of the Gospel anywhere in the world.

Final Remarks

References

American Psychiatric Association (2013) *Diagnostic and Statistical Manual of mental Disorders*, 5th Edition, Arlington, VA, APA publishing

Arbuckle, G.A. (1996) *From Chaos to Mission: Reforming Religious Life Formation*, London, Geoffrey Chapman

Aschenbrenner, G.A. (2002) *Quickening the Fire in our Midst: the Challenge of Diocesan Priestly Spirituality*, Chicago, Loyola Press

Azevedo, M (1998) *Vocation for Mission*, New York: Paulist Press

Barrett, W (1958) *The Irrational Man*, New York, Doubleday

Benedict XVI (2005), *Deus Caritas Est*, Encyclical, December 25.

_____ (2006) "It is all about being with Christ", Address to the bishops, priests and deacons at Freising, Germany, September 14.

Berger, P.L & Luckmann, T (1966) *The Social Construction of Reality*, New York, Anchor Books

CBCN (2004), *I Chose You; The Nigerian Priest in the Third Millennium*, Abuja, Publication of the Catholic Secretariat

_____ (2005) *Ratio Fundamentalis Institutionis Sacerdotalis*, Abuja, Publication of the Catholic Secretariat

Coleman, G. D (2002) "Human Sexuality and Priestly Formation", *Seminary Journal*, 8/1, 16-23.

Congregation for Catholic Education (2008) *Guidelines for the Use of Psychology in the Admission and Formation of Candidates for the Priesthood*, June 28.

Dolan, T.M. (2000) *Priests for the Third Millennium*, Huntington, Our Sunday Visitor, Inc.

Ebigbo, P.O, Janakiramaiah, N & Kumaraswamy, N. (1989) "Somatization in Cross-Cultural Perspective" in Peltzer, K. & Ebigbo, P.O. (eds.) *Clinical Psychology in Africa: South of the Sahara, the Caribbean & Afro-Latin America*, Enugu, Nigeria, Chuka Printing Co. 233-249.

Glasser, W. (1998) *Choice Theory: A New Psychology of Personal Freedom*, New York, NY, HarperCollins Publishers Inc.

Grant, T (1995) *The Silence of Unknowing: The Key to the Spiritual Life*, Liguori, Missouri, Triumph Books.

Hahn, S (2002) *First Comes Love: Finding your Family in the Church and the Trinity*, New York, Doubleday.

Häring, B (1989) *Priesthood Imperiled: A Critical Examination of Ministry in the Catholic Church*, Liguori, Missouri, Triumph Books.

Ihezue, U.H (1989) "The Influence of Sociocultural Factors on Symptoms of Depressive Illness" in Ebigbo, P.O, Janakiramaiah, N & Kumaraswamy, N (eds.) *Clinical Psychology in Africa: South of the Sahara, the Caribbean & Afro-Latin America*, Enugu- Nigeria, Chuka Printing Co.

Ike, O (1993) "The Priest in the Modern World: Inadequacies in the Priestly Formation in the Context of Nigeria", in *Symposium,* Queen of Apostle Seminary, Imezi-Owa, Nigeria, original copy.

John Paul II, (1992) Post-Synodal Apostolic Exhortation, *Pastores Dabo Vobis* on the Formation of Priests in the Circumstances of the Present day.

_____ (1995) Post-Synodal Apostolic Exhortation, *Eccleasia in Africa* on the Church in Africa and its Evangelizing Mission towards the year 2000.

_____ (1996) Post-Synodal Apostolic Exhortation, *Vita Consacrata,* on the Consecrated Life.

_____ (1994) *Crossing the Threshold of Hope* trans. New York, Random House.

Kiechle, S. (2005) *The Art of Discernment: Making Good Decisions in your World of Choices,* Notre Dame, Indiana, Ave Maria Press.

Kiely, B (1987) *Psychology and Moral Theology,* Rome, Pontifical Gregorian University Press

_____ (1997) "Dialettica di Base: Desiderio, Limite e Dono di Sé", in *Atti: 3° Convegno di Studio, L'Accompagnamento,* 36-46, unpublished.

Maloney, F.J. (1980) *Disciples and Prophets: A Biblical Model for the Religious Life,* New York, Crossroad.

Manenti, A. (1988) *Vivere ghi Ideali: frap aura e Desiderio/1,* Bologna, Edizione Bologna.

Manturana, H.R. & Varela, F.J (1987) *The Tree of Knowledge: the Biological Roots of Human Understanding*, rev. ed. Boston, Shambhala Publications Inc.

Mbiti, J.S. (1969) *African Religions and Philosophy*, London Heinemann Educational books.

Martini (1992) *Abraham our Father in Faith*, trans. India, Gujarat Sahitya Prakash.

Newberg, A & Waldman M.R, ((2006) *Why we believe what we believe: Uncovering our Biological need for Meaning, Spirituality and Truth*, New York, Free Press.

Nouwen, H (1989) *In the Name of Jesus: Reflections on Christian Leadership*, London, Darton, Longman & Todd.

Nuttin, J (1985) *Future Time Perspective and Motivation: Theory and Research Method*, trans. rev. ed. Leuven, Leuven University Press & Lawrence Erlbaum Associates Inc.

Nwagwu, M.G (1993) "Religious Life in Nigeria Today", in *AFER* 35/4, 222-239.

Obiefuna, A.K (1985) *Idolatry in a Century-old Faith*, Lenten pastoral.

_____ (1993) "Presenting *Pastores Dabo Vobis* to the Nigerian Priests and Seminarians", in *Symposium*, Queen of Apostle Seminary, Imezi-Owa, Nigeria, 1993. Original copy

O'Dwyer, C (2000) *Imagining One's Future: A Projective Approach to Christian Maturity*, Doctoral Dissertation, Rome, Pontifical Gregorian University Press.

O'Murchu, D (1999) *Poverty, Celibacy, and Obedience*, New York, Crossroad.

Okeke, C.U (2003) *Expectations of Life as a Priest: a Comparative Study of Igbo Diocesan and Religious Seminarians,* Doctoral Dissertation, Rome, Pontifical Gregorian University Press.

_____ (2009) "The Charism and Spirituality of Diocesan Priests", Homily given to the Awka Diocesan Priests on their recollection day, 4th November 2009.

_____ (2006) *The Future of Catholic Priesthood in Igboland: Dangers and Challenges Ahead*, Nimo, Rex Charles Ltd; reprinted in 2015 in Abuja by GiPi, Publications.

_____ (2007) *I am Married but Lonely: Issues in Marital Loneliness and Intimacy*, Nimo, Rex Charles Ltd; Reprinted in 2015 in Abuja by GiPi publications

_____ (2008) *On Being a Fulfilled Catholic Priest: Understanding the Experience of Meaning and Meaninglessness in the Priesthood*, Nimo, Rex Charles Ltd; reprinted in 2015 in Abuja by GiPi publications

Rausch, T.P (1992) *Priesthood Today: an Appraisal*, New York, New Jersey, Paulist Press

Ronco, A (1994) "Formazione umana di Base del Futuro Pastore", in dal Covolo, E & Triacca A.M (eds.) *Sacerdoti per la nuova evangelizazzione*, Las-Roma, Librería atebei Salesiano.

Rossetti, S.J (1999) "Understanding Diocesan Priesthood", in *Human Development* 20/1, 35-39.

_____ (2011) *Why Priests are Happy: A Study of the Psychological and Spiritual Health of Priests*, Notre Dame, Indiana, Ave Maria Press.

Rulla, L.M ((1986) *Anthropology of Christian Vocation: Interdisciplinary Bases,* vol. 1, Rome, Pontifical Gregorian University Press.

Shineller, P. (1990) *A Handibook on Inculturation*, New York-Mahwah, Paulist Press.

_____ (2001) "The Architecture of Seminaries", in *Seminary Journal*, 7/1, 44-49.

Shorter, A (1997) "The Family as a Model for Social Reconstruction in Africa", in *Theology of the Church as Family of God*, Tangaza Occasional papers/3, Nairobi, Pauline Publications Africa.

Smith, W. C (1979)) *Faith and Belief: the Difference Between them*, Oxford, One World

Synod of Bishops (1990) on the Formation of Priests in the Circumstances of Today, *Lineamenta* nos. 25-26; *Instrumentum Laboris*, nos. 22, 23, 30.

Totaro, D (2005) *My Just One shall live by Faith*, Benin City-Nigeria, Luckbee Press.

Vanier, J (1998) *Becoming Human*, Toronto, Canadian Broadcasting Cooperation.

Vergote, A (1999) "Psicologia dell'identità religiosa: struttura, processi, problem", in Aletti, M & Rossi (eds.) *Ricerca di Sé e transcendenza*, Torino, Centro Scientifico editore.

De Waal, E (1989) *Living with Contradiction: An Introduction to Benedictine Spirituality*, New York, Morehouse.

Wolff, P (2003) *Discernment: the Art of Choosing Well*, rev. ed. Liguori, Missouri, Triumph books.

Other books by the author

*The Future of Catholic Priesthood in Igboland:
    The Dangers and Challenges Ahead

*On Being a Fulfilled Catholic Priest

*Love: with or without sex?

*I am Married but Lonely:
    Issues in Marital Loneliness and Intimacy

*When Love runs Dry

www.ingramcontent.com/pod-product-compliance
Lightning Source LLC
Chambersburg PA
CBHW071122280326
41935CB00010B/1089